Lacey M. Sloan, PhD
Nora S. Gustavsson, PhD
Editors

Violence and Social Injustice Against Lesbian, Gay and Bisexual People

Violence and Social Injustice Against Lesbian, Gay and Bisexual People has been co-published simultaneously as *Journal of Gay & Lesbian Social Services*, Volume 8, Number 3 1998.

Pre-publication
REVIEWS,
COMMENTARIES,
EVALUATIONS . . .

" . . . [A]n important and timely book that exposes the multilevel nature of violence against gay, lesbian, bisexual, and transgendered people. It challenges the reader by illustrating multifaceted links between violence and injustice and analyzing root causes. By drawing attention to the intersectionality of multiple oppressions, the book's collection of articles illustrates how interpersonal, intrapersonal, and collective violence keeps diverse gay men and lesbians at the margin economically, politically, socially, and personally."

Dorothy Van Soest, DSW
Associate Dean
School of Social Work
University of Texas at Austin

Violence and Social Injustice Against Lesbian, Gay and Bisexual People

Violence and Social Injustice Against Lesbian, Gay and Bisexual People has been co-published as *Journal of Gay & Lesbian Social Services*, Volume 8, Number 3 1998.

Violence and Social Injustice Against Lesbian, Gay and Bisexual People

Lacey M. Sloan, PhD
Nora S. Gustavsson, PhD
Editors

Violence and Social Injustice, edited by Lacey M. Sloan and Nora S. Gustavsson, was previously issued by The Haworth Press, Inc., under the same title, as special issues of *Journal of Gay & Lesbian Social Servicesy*, Volume 8, Number 3 1998, James J. Kelly, Editor.

Harrington Park Press
An Imprint of
The Haworth Press, Inc.
New York • London

122-X

Published by

Harrington Park Press, 10 Alice Street, Binghamton, NY 13904-1580

Harrington Park Press is an Imprint of the Haworth Press, Inc., 10 Alice Street, Binghamton, Ny 13904-1580 USA.

Violence and Social Injustice Against Lesbian, Gay and Bisexual People has been co-published as *Journal of Gay & Lesbian Social Services*™, Volume 8, Number 3 1998.

The Haworth Press, Inc., 10 Alice Street, Binghamton, NY 13904-1580 USA

Library of Congress Cataloging-in-Publication Data

Violence and social injustice against lesbian, gay and bisexual people / Lacey M. Sloan, Nora S. Gustavsson, editors.
    p. cm.
    Co-published simultaneously as Journal of gay & lesbian social services, volume 8, number 3, 1998.
    Includes bibliographical references (p.) and index.
    ISBN 0-7890-0650-2 (alk. paper) – ISBN 1-56023-122-X (alk. paper)
    1. Gay men–Crimes against. 2. Lesbians–Crimes against. 3. Bisexuals–Crimes against. 4. Social justice. 5. Discrimination. I. Sloan, Lacey M. II. Gustavsson, Nora S. III. Journal of gay & lesbian social services, v. 8, no. 3.

HV6250.4.H66V56 1998
364.1–dc21
                                      98-38651
                                        CIP

INDEXING & ABSTRACTING

Contributions to this publication are selectively indexed or abstracted in print, electronic, online, or CD-ROM version(s) of the reference tools and information services listed below. This list is current as of the copyright date of this publication. See the end of this section for additional notes.

- *AIDS Newsletter c/o CAB International/CAB ACCESS . . . available in print, diskettes updated weekly, and on INTERNET. Providing full bibliographic listings, author affiliation, augmented keyword searching,* CAB International, P.O. Box 100,Wallingford Oxon OX10 8DE, United Kingdom

- *Cambridge Scientific Abstracts, Risk Abstracts,* 7200 Wisconsin Avenue #601, Bethesda, MD 20814

- *caredata CD: the social and community care database,* National Institute for Social Work, 5 Tavistock Place, London WC1H 9SS, England

- *CNPIEC Reference Guide: Chinese National Directory of Foreign Periodicals,* P.O. Box 88, Beijing, People's Republic of China

- *Contemporary Women's Issues,* Responsive Databases Services, 23611 Chagrin Blvd., Suite 320, Beachwood, OH 44122

- *Criminal Justice Abstracts,* Willow Tree Press, 15 Washington Street, 4th Floor, Newark, NJ 07102

- *Digest of Neurology and Psychiatry,* The Institute of Living, 400 Washington Street, Hartford, CT 06106

- *ERIC Clearinghouse on Urban Education (ERIC/CUE),* Teachers College, Columbia University, Box 40, New York, NY 10027

- *Family Studies Database (online and CD/ROM),* National Information Services Corporation, 306 East Baltimore Pike, 2nd Floor, Media, PA 19063

- *HOMODOK/"Relevant" Bibliographic Database,* Documentation Centre for Gay & Lesbian Studies, University of Amsterdam (selective printed abstracts in "Homologie" and bibliographic computer databases covering cultural, historical, social and political aspects of gay & lesbian topics), c/o HOMODOK-ILGA Archive, O. Z. Achterburgwal 185, NL-1012 DK, Amsterdam, The Netherlands

(continued)

- *IBZ International Bibliography of Periodical Literature,* Zeller Verlag GmbH & Co., P.O.B. 1949, d-49009 Osnabruck, Germany

- *Index to Periodical Articles Related to Law,* University of Texas, 727 East 26th Street, Austin, TX 78705

- *INTERNET ACCESS (& additional networks) Bulletin Board for Libraries ("BUBL"), coverage of information resources on INTERNET, JANET, and other networks.*
    - <URL:http://bubl.ac.uk/>
    - The new locations will be found under <URL:http://bubl.ac.uk/link/>.
    - Any existing BUBL users who have problems finding information on the new service should contact the BUBL help line by sending e-mail to <bubl@bubl.ac.uk>.
  The Andersonian Library, Curran Building, 101 St. James Road, Glasgow G4 0NS, Scotland

- *Mental Health Abstracts (online through DIALOG),* IFI/Plenum Data Company, 3202 Kirkwood Highway, Wilmington, DE 19808

- *Referativnyi Zhurnal (Abstracts Journal of the All-Russian Institute of Scientific and Technical Information),* 20 Usievich Street, Moscow 125219, Russia

- *Social Work Abstracts,* National Association of Social Workers, 750 First Street NW, 8th Floor, Washington, DC 20002

- *Sociological Abstracts (SA),* Sociological Abstracts, Inc., P.O. Box 22206, San Diego, CA 92192-0206

- *Studies on Women Abstracts,* Carfax Publishing Company, P.O. Box 25, Abingdon, Oxon OX14 3UE, United Kingdom

- *Violence and Abuse Abstracts: A Review of Current Literature on Interpersonal Violence (VAA),* Sage Publications, Inc., 2455 Teller Road, Newbury Park, CA 91320

- *Women "R" CD/ROM,* Softline Information, Inc., 20 Summer Street, Stamford, CT 06901. A new full text Windows Database on CD/ROM. Presents full depth coverage of the wide range of subjects that impact and reflect the lives of women. Can be reached at 1 (800) 524-7922, www.slinfo.com, or e-mail: hoch@slinfo.com

(continued)

SPECIAL BIBLIOGRAPHIC NOTES

related to special journal issues (separates)
and indexing/abstracting

☐ indexing/abstracting services in this list will also cover material in any "separate" that is co-published simultaneously with Haworth's special thematic journal issue or DocuSerial. Indexing/abstracting usually covers material at the article/chapter level.

☐ monographic co-editions are intended for either non-subscribers or libraries which intend to purchase a second copy for their circulating collections.

☐ monographic co-editions are reported to all jobbers/wholesalers/approval plans. The source journal is listed as the "series" to assist the prevention of duplicate purchasing in the same manner utilized for books-in-series.

☐ to facilitate user/access services all indexing/abstracting services are encouraged to utilize the co-indexing entry note indicated at the bottom of the first page of each article/chapter/contribution.

☐ this is intended to assist a library user of any reference tool (whether print, electronic, online, or CD-ROM) to locate the monographic version if the library has purchased this version but not a subscription to the source journal.

☐ individual articles/chapters in any Haworth publication are also available through the Haworth Document Delivery Service (HDDS).

CONTENTS

ABOUT THE EDITORS

Lacey M. Sloan, PhD, is Assistant Professor in the Graduate School of Social Work at the University of Houston. Currently, Dr. Sloan serves as President of the Texas Association Against Sexual Assault (TAASA) and as a board member for the Montrose Counseling Center. Dr. Sloan has presented papers at conferences in several national and international forums, and has published articles and contributions in numerous journals and books, including the *Journal of Gay & Lesbian Social Services* (The Haworth Press, Inc.), *Journal of Medicine and Law*, and *Journal of Social Work*, and *Social Work: Issues and Opportunities in a Challenging Profession* (Prentice-Hall, 1997). Her current research focuses on sexual violence; sex work; oppression and social justice; and lesbian, gay, and bisexual issues.

Nora S. Gustavsson, PhD, is Associate Professor in the School of Social Work at Arizona State University in Tempe. Dr. Gustavsson's research focuses on vulnerable populations, and her publications have appeared in journals, edited books, and a textbook on child welfare policy. Her recent articles have addressed questions about the role of the Indian Child Welfare Act in protecting Indian children, drug use by pregnant and parenting women, creative strategies for combining the roles of practitioner and researcher, and pedagogy. She teaches policy and practice at all three levels of social work education.

Foreword

In a book review written recently for the *New York Times*, Susan Jacoby described an exhibit she saw at the Metropolitan Museum of Art. She tells of an icon depicting souls struggling to climb a ladder to heaven, while below them demons wait gleefully to capture any who happen to fall (Jacoby, 1997). When I read the articles in this collection, I could not erase the image of that icon from my mind's eye.

The articles in this volume relate the struggles of gay, lesbian, bisexual, and transgendered people against injustice and violence in their lives. As Steven Onken points out in the first article, we usually think of violence against gay, lesbian, bisexual, and transgendered people in terms of street violence–attacks by insecure, hypermasculine adolescent thugs. This doesn't deny the harm done, but it does make the violence more anomolous, easier to explain away. But Onken emphasizes that the violence is all around us: in laws banning same-sex marriages and criminalizing homosexual acts; in military regulations that require gay, lesbian, bisexual, and transgendered people to hide who they are and deny themselves companionship and sexual fulfillment; in employment and housing discrimination; in hostile schools that render homosexuals invisible in the curriculum, the classroom, and the student body. And, Onken rightly argues, all of these types of violence are interrelated; indeed, they feed on each other.

Denial is also a theme in Sloan, King, and Sheppard's article, which focuses on the content of training materials used to educate and sensitize law enforcement officers about hate crimes. In a survey of police officials responsible for hate crime record keeping, Sloan et al. were met with what to me were familiar responses when they asked specifically about hate crimes against gays and lesbians: "It's not a problem here," "It's not our problem," or "We'll get to it later; it's not as important as other issues."

[Haworth co-indexing entry note]: "Foreword." Renzetti, Claire. Co-published simultaneously in *Journal of Gay & Lesbian Social Services* (The Haworth Press, Inc.) Vol. 8, No. 3, 1998, pp. xv-xviii; and: *Violence and Social Injustice Against Lesbian, Gay and Bisexual People* (ed: Lacey M. Sloan and Nora S. Gustavsson) The Haworth Press, Inc., 1998, pp. xiii-xvi. Single or multiple copies of this article are available for a fee from The Haworth Document Delivery Service [1-800-342-9678, 9:00 a.m. - 5:00 p.m. (EST). E-mail address: getinfo@haworthpressinc.com].

Several years ago when I surveyed domestic violence agencies about the services available to lesbian victims of partner abuse, I was frequently told that no services were needed: no lesbians ever presented as victims of domestic violence (Renzetti, 1996). Of course, the question that Saulnier raised is apropos here: How do they know they have never had lesbian clients? Moreover, notice that denial of the problem serves the useful purpose of making it go away–or at least remain out of sight to those who must address it, be they police, clinicians, or domestic violence agencies.

In addition to gays and lesbians of color, youth, in particular, are rendered powerless in our society. Ironically, social services ostensibly designed to "protect" them often inflict greater harm, either through benign neglect or outright repression. Gustavsson and MacEachron, for example, point out that school could be "safe space" for gay, lesbian, bisexual, and transgendered youth, but instead it is usually a site of harassment, where at best homosexual, bisexual, and transgendered youth are made to feel unwelcome, or worse, are intentionally victimized by teachers as well as peers.

Saulnier extends this discussion by looking at the problem of suicidality and other social and mental health problems of gay, lesbian, bisexual, and transgendered youth. Saulnier alerts us to some of the serious methodological weaknesses in research on suicidality, pointing out that virtually all the studies rely on nonrandom clinical samples which are hardly representative of the homosexual, bisexual, and transgendered populations. I have raised this methodological issue, too, regarding research on same-sex partner abuse (Renzetti, 1992). As long as gays, lesbians, bisexuals, and transgendered people are stigmatized, it will remain impossible for researchers to select truly random and, therefore, representative samples. In the meantime, the best available data indicate that gay, lesbian, bisexual, and transgendered youth are at disproportionate risk for suicidality and other mental health problems, but as Saulnier shows, they are unlikely to receive the professional help they need. Practitioners and clinicians frequently maintain that they have no gay or lesbian clients because they assume they'd "know one when they see one" and they haven't seen one.

One of the major strengths of this publication, in fact, is its attention to the intersectionality of multiple oppressions. As Dorie Gilbert Martinez states in her article, we must begin to see the oppression of gay, lesbian, bisexual, and transgendered people through a prism, rather than the single lens of oppression. To this end, readers will find the concerns of racial and ethnic minorities and young people well represented in these pages.

Martinez discusses how for all gays and lesbians coming out is a daily process, but the point is especially salient for minority gays and lesbians because they must negotiate multiple worlds–the world of straights, their own communities of color, and the gay and lesbian community–each of which may prove hostile, but for different reasons. Of special value in Martinez's article is her attention to the ways that social class inequality often intersects with heterosexism and racism. She points out, for instance, that discrimination against gays and lesbians in the military is of particular concern to gays and lesbians of color because of the increasing number of racial and ethnic minorities entering the military as a means of economic survival. Martinez also states that Latina lesbians are sometimes marginalized within the gay and lesbian community because of their working class status.

Flavio Francisco Marsiglia takes up a related issue. He argues that practitioners and academics must begin to look at the central role that ethnicity and culture play in the formation of sexual identities. Marsiglia makes the important point that there is no such thing as a "culture-free" or "ethnic-free" lesbian or gay identity. For gays and lesbians of color, racial/ethnic identity is integrated with sexual identity, and this integration not infrequently generates a subculture of resistance to oppression on both fronts.

Lest I leave you with the impression that there is no good news in the pages that follow, I draw your attention to the articles by Anastas and Kopels. Both authors discuss legislation or pending legal action designed to prohibit discrimination on the basis of sexual orientation–Anastas with respect to employment and Kopels with respect to marriage. Nevertheless, both authors also examine the difficulties of enforcement. Anastas writes of the "lavender ceiling" that gays and lesbians encounter in many workplaces. She also shows how homophobia gets translated into a justification for discrimination: The idea that "the presence of gays and lesbians disrupts the workplace so they shouldn't be permitted there" effectively turns the tables so that the discriminator's problem (homophobia) is made the problem of those discriminated against (disruptiveness).

Kopels discusses the more controversial topic of same-sex marriage, a topic that has proved divisive not only outside the gay and lesbian community, but also within it. There are those who believe that the legalization of same-sex marriage is the best way to guarantee gay and lesbian couples all the rights and benefits that are currently bestowed on opposite-sex couples when they marry. Others, however, question the efficacy of embracing the repressive institution of marriage, and they worry that the legalization of same-sex marriage will establish a false dichtomy between "good" gays and lesbians (i.e., those in long-term monogamous relationships) and "bad" (or "promiscuous" uncoupled) gays and lesbians (Duggan, 1997;

Robson, 1992). Kopels tells us, however, that even if the battle for same-sex marriage is won in *Baehr v. Lewin,* other states have already taken steps to ensure that any marriages of gay and lesbian couples performed in Hawaii will not be legally recognized elsewhere.

There has certainly been a good deal of activism nationally, especially by the radical right, to prevent the legalization of same-sex marriages. And Kopels's article raised red flags for me, warning of the dangers to the community if it becomes polarized over this issue. Of course, the debate, while heated, is hardly as simplistic as I've presented it here. But while we argue the fine points, the radical right is mobilizing to deny gay, lesbian, bisexual, and transgendered people as many rights as possible even as progress is made on some fronts to secure particular rights and benefits. I envision a protracted battle, with the justice struggles described in these pages being fought far longer than any of us would wish. Behold the demons, but don't dare let go of the ladder.

Claire Renzetti

REFERENCES

Duggan, L. (1997). Queering the family: Beyond the marriage juggernaut. Paper presented at *Relatively Speaking: A Conference on Lesbian, Gay, Bisexual and Transgendered Families.* New York.

Jacoby, S. (1997). The permanently poor. *New York Times Book Review. May 4.* 10-12.

Renzetti, C. M. (1992). *Violent betrayal: Partner abuse in lesbian relationships.* Thousand Oaks, CA: Sage Publications.

Robson, R. (1992). *Lesbian (out)law.* Ithaca, NY: Firebrand Books.

Introduction

Nora S. Gustavsson
Lacey M. Sloan

At first glance, some readers may be surprised by the range of articles in this special edition. When we think about violence, we usually think primarily about interpersonal violence. Certainly, domestic violence is a worthy topic for exploration and concern, but one that is the topic of a special issue of the *Journal of Gay & Lesbian Social Services.* Fewer people may be cognizant of the many varied expressions of violence that do not involve physical acts of harm. It is these expressions of violence and social injustice that we address in this collection.

The hatred of sexual minority persons[1] results in many forms of violence and acts of social injustice directed toward lesbian, gay, bisexual, and transgendered people, including hate crimes, sexual harassment, discrimination, economic injustice, denial of civil rights, and heterosexist social services. Sexual minority persons who internalize these negative messages into self-hatred may participate in self-destructive behavior such as chemical abuse and suicide. Sexual minority persons who come out may be rejected by their families, forced out of their homes, or harassed by their peers. Social institutions such as public schools can contribute to a hostile environment in which gay, lesbian, and bisexual youth are placed at an elevated risk for educational failure and emotional and physical violence.

The goal of this volume is to explore the multiple forms of violence experienced by lesbian, gay, bisexual, and transgendered people. We offer readers the following definition of violence:

---

1. For the purposes of this article, sexual minority refers to lesbian, gay, bisexual, and transgendered persons.

[Haworth co-indexing entry note]: "Introduction." Gustavsson, Nora S., and Lacey M. Sloan. Co-published simultaneously in *Journal of Gay & Lesbian Social Services* (The Haworth Press, Inc.) Vol. 8, No. 3, 1998, pp. 1-4; and: *Violence and Social Injustice Against Lesbian, Gay and Bisexual People* (ed: Lacey M. Sloan, and Nora S. Gustavsson) The Haworth Press, Inc., 1998, pp. 1-4. Single or multiple copies of this article are available for a fee from The Haworth Document Delivery Service [1-800-342-9678, 9:00 a.m. - 5:00 p.m. (EST). E-mail address: getinfo@haworthpressinc.com].

Broadly, any act, whether overt or covert, that coerces or causes physical hurt, material loss or mental anguish, or that degrades human beings or that militates against human rights, dignity, and decency should be viewed as an act of violence. (Rajgopal, 1987, p. 5)

Violence is by its very nature ubiquitous and is perpetrated by the state, institutions, organizations and individuals. This collection highlights the political, economic, and social manifestations of violence directed against sexual minority persons. This environmental approach to violence places responsibility for violence on the institutions and organizations of contemporary American society and seeks to avoid blaming the victim of the violence.

In our society, lesbians, gay men, bisexuals, and transgendered persons are still considered by some to be immoral, unnatural, and/or dysfunctional. Until 1973, homosexuality was defined as a mental illness by the American Psychiatric Association's Diagnostic and Statistical Manual (DSM) (APA, 1952). Frequently, "treatment" to change a person's sexual orientation occurred whether or not the individual wanted to change his or her sexual orientation. The decision to remove homosexuality from the DSM was hailed as an important achievement by gay rights groups and others who had fought for its removal. Nonetheless, negative attitudes towards sexual minority persons continue.

Lesbians, gay men, bisexuals and transgendered persons do not have civil and statutory protection under the law (Title VII of the 1964 Civil Rights Act) (Herek & Berrill, 1992). In fact, government is taking a leading role in the subjugation of lesbians and gays by denying legal recognition of same sex unions. Benefits that most heterosexuals take for granted are denied to lesbian, gay, bisexual and transgendered persons in same sex relationships. For example, same sex partners cannot marry in any state in the United States, although this has been challenged recently. Sexual acts between consenting adults of the same sex is illegal in over half of the states. Lesbian and gay parents have lost custody of their children when their sexual orientation became known. Unless a power of attorney has provided authorization or biological relatives permit, same sex partners may not make medical decisions or even funeral arrangements for their partner.

Homophobia and heterosexism has inhibited service delivery to lesbians, gay men, bisexuals and transgendered persons (Morrow, 1993). Social service agencies that are feminist and gay-supportive may fear losing funding if services are explicitly offered and advertised for the lesbian and gay community. The lack of truly accessible (i.e., supportive, gay-friendly, gay-appropriate) social services results in this population underutilizing services available to the general population.

We must also understand the interconnection of all oppression. The historical antipathy between ethnic minority and sexual minority communities only serves the interest of those who seek to oppress both groups. Persons of color who come out may be rejected by their ethnic culture, and still face racism within the gay community. As long as any group is oppressed or devalued, violence against those persons may be tolerated, if not supported, by society. The diversity of the gay community must be acknowledged, embraced, and valued.

Changes in the environment seem to be occurring. Lesbian and gay groups have begun to change and overturn laws and policies that have negatively impacted them. Many companies, some states and municipalities are beginning to extend insurance benefits to same sex partners (also known as domestic partnerships). Sodomy and homosexual sex laws have been repealed or overturned in many states. Lesbians and gay men are asserting their right to marry through religious or private, non-civil ceremonies. Law enforcement is becoming more active in some communities; for example, the Houston, Texas Police Department has conducted undercover operations to curb incidents of "gay bashing."

Some social workers have noted that the profession has hardly been at the forefront of advocacy for lesbians, gay men, and bisexuals. Sexual minority persons, even in a field alleged to be as liberal as social work, can find themselves victims of discrimination in the workplace. Nonetheless, in recent years the profession has taken a number of actions to affirm its commitment to lesbian, gay, bisexual, and transgendered persons. The revised Code of Ethics of the National Association of Social Workers (NASW) contains the following statement supporting sexual minority persons:

> The social worker should not practice, condone, facilitate or collaborate with any form of discrimination on the basis of race, color, sexual orientation, age, religion, national origin, marital status, political belief, mental or physical handicap, or any other preference or personal characteristic, condition or status. (1996, p. 33)

There is still much violence and social injustice that must be overcome before lesbian, gay, bisexual, and transgendered persons are able to enjoy the full benefits of our society. Social workers must work to end the oppression and discrimination of lesbian, gay, bisexual, and transgendered persons. Although social work may not have been at the forefront of the gay rights movement, the profession has clearly moved toward a position in support of the rights of lesbian, gay, bisexual, and transgendered persons. We must work for the adoption of civil and statutory protection for sexual minority persons. We must combat homophobia and heterosexism in our culture.

It is our hope that this special publication will contribute to affirming the lives of sexual minority persons by alerting the readers to the insidious nature of violence and social injustice. It is time to stop the violence and create a world that is socially just for all members of our society.

REFERENCES

American Psychological Association (APA). (1952). *Diagnostic and statistical manual: Mental disorders*. Washington, DC: Author.

Herek, G. M., & Berrill, K. T. (1992). *Hate crimes: Confronting violence against lesbians and gay men*. Newbury Park, CA: Sage Publications.

Morrow, D. (1993). Social work with gay and lesbian adolescents. *Social Work, 38*(6), 655-660.

National Association of Social Workers (NASW). (1996). *Code of ethics of the National Association of Social Workers*. (Available from NASW, 750 First Street, NE, Suite 700, Washington, DC 20002-4241).

VIOLENCE

Conceptualizing Violence Against Gay, Lesbian, Bisexual, Intersexual, and Transgendered People

Steven J. Onken

SUMMARY. This article provides a conceptual model for defining antigay violence that incorporates the diverse manifestations of such violence, its multilevel nature, and its structural and ideological foundations. Interconnections are made among oppression, power, moral exclusion, and stigmatization. In particular, the impact of heterosexist oppression, including its roots in the moral and medical paradigms, and gender oppression are explored. *[Article copies available for a fee from The Haworth Document Delivery Service: 1-800-342-9678. E-mail address: getinfo@haworthpressinc.com]*

Steven J. Onken, MSSW-AP, is a doctoral candidate at the School of Social Work, The University of Texas at Austin, 1925 San Jacinto Boulevard, Austin, TX 78712-1203. The author wishes to express his appreciation to Dorothy Van Soest for her encouragement and guidance in the completion of this article.

[Haworth co-indexing entry note]: "Conceptualizing Violence Against Gay, Lesbian, Bisexual, Intersexual, and Transgendered People." Onken, Steven J. Co-published simultaneously in *Journal of Gay & Lesbian Social Services* (The Haworth Press, Inc.) Vol. 8, No. 3, 1998, pp. 5-24; and: *Violence and Social Injustice Against Lesbian, Gay and Bisexual People* (ed: Lacey M. Sloan, and Nora S. Gustavsson) The Haworth Press, Inc., 1998, pp. 5-24. Single or multiple copies of this article are available for a fee from The Haworth Document Delivery Service [1-800-342-9678, 9:00 a.m. - 5:00 p.m. (EST). E-mail address: getinfo@haworthpressinc.com].

National statistics document that antigay[1] hate crime is increasing and that these violent incidents are becoming more brutal (Gallagher, 1995; Singer & Deschamps, 1994). Under organized pressure from gay constituents and allies from other marginalized groups affected by hate crimes, an increasing number of federal, state, and local entities have responded with hate crime legislation, hate crime prosecution, and antiviolence programs. But most forms of violence directed at the sexual minority populations,[2] i.e., gay men, lesbians, and intersexual,[3] bisexual, and transgendered[4] people, are submerged from view. These forms of violence often go unchallenged and are viewed with indifference or are considered legitimate and acceptable (Van Soest & Bryant, 1995).

This article provides a conceptual model that incorporates the diverse manifestations of antigay violence, its multilevel nature, and its structural and ideological foundations. Interconnections are made among oppression, power, moral exclusion, and stigmatization. In particular, the impact of heterosexist oppression, including its roots in the moral and medical paradigms, and gender oppression are explored.

CONCEPTUALIZING VIOLENCE

Through a synthesis of several theoretical perspectives, Van Soest and Bryant (1995) conceptualized a model of violence that identified the multiple manifestations of violence, its multilevel nature, and the oppression inherent in all levels. Citing Bulhan (1985) and Salmi (1993), they defined violence "as any act or situation in which a person injures another, including both direct attacks on a person's physical or psychological integrity and destructive actions that do not involve a direct relationship between the victims and the perpetrators" (Van Soest & Bryant, 1995, p. 550). This definition "emphasizes the consequences from the victim's perspective" (p. 550); treats individual, group, institutional, and societal violence equally; includes socially sanctioned, unintended, nonphysical, subtle, covert, and long-term consequential forms of violence; and "includes any avoidable action that violates a human right in the broadest sense or that prevents the fulfillment of a basic human need" (p. 550).

Levels of Violence

Van Soest and Bryant's (1995) conceptualization incorporates three levels of violence: (1) individual–"harmful acts against people or property" (p. 550), (2) institutional–"harmful actions by social institutions and their various organizational units that obstruct the spontaneous unfolding of human potential" (p. 551), and (3) structural-cultural–"the normative and ideological roots of violence that undergird and give rise to the institutional and individual levels" (p. 551). The third level, structural-cultural, tends to be the most invisible as it is so ingrained into society's infrastructure that it is taken for granted as fact or "the ways things are." Efforts to identify and question these ideological roots of violence are viewed as threats to social order, undermining the traditional normative family and community. These three levels of violence are readily apparent in society's and the general population's treatment of gay, lesbian, bisexual, intersexual, and transgendered people.

Structural-cultural level. North American and much of "Western societal" traditional views and beliefs hold that people who constitute the sexual minorities are defective, pathological and/or abominable. These beliefs have been derived from and reinforced by moral and medical models (or paradigms) embedded in how professions and the general public "cope with" and control societal members who are deemed too sexually different and of little worth. The moral and medical models sanction and reinforce a structural-cultural social order exclusively based on heterosexuality. This social order is, in turn, further sanctioned and reinforced by traditional notions of gender, that is, what constitutes a healthy, normal man or woman. The current patriarchal hierarchy of US society is heavily invested in maintaining these beliefs and ideologies to prevent potential undermining of the existing social order. Much of the remainder of this article will explore these ideologies and the resulting oppression and violence.

Institutional level. Kirk and Madsen (1989) identify classes of institutional actions by which heterosexuals express hatred of gay people in US society. These can be expanded to the entire sexual minority population and track Van Soest and Bryant's institutional levels of violence. These actions outlaw homosexual, bisexual, and transgendered behavior per se and are orchestrated by government at local, state, and national levels in the form of laws which criminalize sex acts commonly associated with homosexuality (usually summarized as "sodomy"–oral/genital sex and/or anal intercourse) as well as court decisions which support those laws. Such laws serve less to prevent gay love-making than to brand it with the government's disapproval, e.g., *Bowers vs. Hardwick* Supreme Court Decision upholding Georgia's sodomy statute.

It is left up to legal, political, and social bureaucracies to apply the government's prejudice in specific, "legalized" ways. They do so through institutional actions that deny or limit sexual minorities their fundamental civil and human rights: actions in which the heterosexual community participates in efforts to limit or keep people who are gay, lesbian, bisexual, intersexual or transgendered from disclosing who they are, speaking, fraternizing, organizing, educating others, working in jobs and residing in neighborhoods they would choose, marrying, parenting, retaining custody of children, reaching out to questioning youth, etc. There are few more serious impediments to personal and collective advancement over the long run than the denial of these rights.

Individual level. It is left up to individual professionals and public citizens to apply the government's prejudice in specific, sanctioned ways. These take the form of actions that otherwise vent public disapproval of sexual minorities: diagnosing and labeling, public taunting (such as that done by public and religious officials, entertainers, and bumper stickers), harassment, and violence–even murder. Autobiographies and collections of narratives of gay, lesbian, bisexual, and transgendered people and their families are filled with accounts of being the target of such violent actions and the resulting immeasurable personal costs (see Aaron, 1995; Barber & Holmes, 1994; Dew, 1994; Feinberg, 1996; Fellows, 1996; Louganis, 1995; Miller, 1989; Monette, 1992; Penelope & Wolfe, 1989; Saks & Curtis, 1994; Sears, 1991; and Tucker, 1995). It merits repeating that hate crime incidents against people who are gay, lesbian, bisexual, and transgendered are on the rise and the attacks are becoming increasingly more savage (Clark, 1996).

Dimensions and Types of Violence

Van Soest and Bryant's (1995) conceptualization of violence also articulates three dimensions of violence relating to perpetrators: (1) interpersonal–"a person or small group doing harm to others," (2) intrapersonal–"a person doing harm to self," and (3) collective–"an organized group or an unorganized mob doing harm to others" (p. 553). Finally, citing Salmi (1993), Van Soest and Bryant identify three types of violence: (1) omission–"failing to help someone in need," (2) repression–"depriving people of their rights," and (3) alienation–"depriving people of self-esteem and identity" (p. 553).

The levels of violence, the dimensions relating to perpetrators, and the types of violence are best understood within the context of how they are intricately interrelated and interlinked. When Dallas Judge Jack Hampton lessened the sentences of men convicted of killing a gay man, as he "[P]ut prostitutes and queers at the same level . . . and I'd be hard-put to give someone life for killing a prostitute" (Singer & Deschamps, 1994), he fostered an institutional act of violence through repression and alienation.

He used the power and authority of his institutional position to give expression to the dominant beliefs and values of society's structural-cultural foundation that the lives of gay people have less value and fewer rights than people who are heterosexual. On an interpersonal dimension Judge Hampton rewarded the convicted killers with lighter sentences, on an intrapersonal dimension his message reinforced self-devaluation among sexual minority individuals vulnerable to such psychological degradation, and on a collective dimension he added to a body of judicial rulings that negatively differentiates the application of fundamental civil and human rights to sexual minority populations.

An example of institutional violence through an act of omission that gave expression to the same dominant and degrading societal values and beliefs, was then-Secretary of Health and Human Service (HHS) Louis Sullivan's 1989 decision to shelve the results of a study HHS had commissioned that found that gay youths were two to three times more likely to attempt suicide than heterosexual youth and that up to 30% of youths who did commit suicide were gay or lesbian (Maguen, 1993). Sullivan's violence of omission had repercussions on the intrapersonal, interpersonal, and collective dimensions as well. In essence, the federal government made a deliberate attempt to withhold findings and recommendations that were of use in helping to keep gay and lesbian youths alive.

This federal action in turn exacerbated states' and local communities' collective failure to identify, acknowledge, and address this critical public health issue. Teachers, psychologists, counselors, and ministers continue to lack the basic information to be of assistance on an interpersonal level to many youths questioning and attempting to come to terms with a sexual identity that is not heterosexual. As for the youths themselves, 18-year-old Vanessa Williams, who seriously considered suicide after being rebuffed in her attempts to get support from school officials, observed that "The message that I get from the federal government is that it's OK to be homophobic and it's OK to gay-bash" (Maguen, 1993, p. 242).

OPPRESSION

Oppression of sexual minority people is inherent throughout the levels, dimensions and types of antigay violence. Oppression is the act of molding, immobilizing, or reducing opportunities which thereby restrains, restricts or prevents social, psychological, and/or economic movement of an individual or a group (Onken, Danis, & Wambach, 1995). Oppression is kept in place by an ideology of superiority and privilege that, in turn, provides the structural-cultural roots and justification for use of institutional and individual levels of violence to ensure the continued existence of that ideology. Simply stated, oppression is an institutionalized, unequal power relationship maintained by violence or the threat of violence. Power becomes a "process whereby individuals or groups gain or maintain the capacity to impose their will upon others through invoking or threatening punishment or through offering or withholding rewards, i.e., controlling resources" (Onken, Danis, & Wambach, 1995, p. 4). In other words, those in power impose their will interpersonally, intrapersonally, and collectively (i.e., the dimensions of violence) through the practices of omission, repression, and alienation (i.e., the types of violence).

Several issues are relevant in understanding the dynamics and mechanics of oppression in regard to sexual minorities. The first involves reinforcing a more sophisticated understanding of oppression through stressing the meaning and unavailability of privilege, that is, exploring the privilege associated with heterosexuality. Another issue involves focusing more on how the seeds of oppression are placed within members of these disadvantaged groups, that is, exploring internalized homophobia, biphobia and other forms of self-hatred. A final consideration focuses on the prevalence of stereotypes and beliefs which make it difficult for gay, lesbian, bisexual, intersexual, and transgendered persons to form alliances with each other and other minority groups.

HETEROSEXISM

Heterosexism is "both the belief that heterosexuality is or should be the only acceptable sexual orientation and the fear and hatred of those who love and sexually desire those of the same sex" (Blumenfeld, 1992, p. 15). The term *homophobia* is often used interchangeably with heterosexism. Homophobia is defined as a fear, usually irrational, of homosexual people based on their sexual orientation including "a prejudice often leading to acts of discrimination, sometimes abusive and violent" (Blumenfeld, 1992, p. 15). Heterosexist beliefs in the superiority and privilege of heterosexuality fuel homophobic behaviors. "Like racism, sexism, and other ideologies of oppression, heterosexism is manifested both in societal customs and institutions, such as religion and the legal system . . . and in individual attitudes and behaviors" (Herek, 1993, p. 221). Anti-gay violence, as evidenced by hate crimes, is a logical, though extreme, extension of the heterosexism that pervades Western society.

Given this common experience of heterosexist oppression, there are major similarities in the histories, life experiences, and civil and social rights movements of persons who make up the sexual minorities. These movements developed in large part as a reaction and rebellion to North American and much of "Western societal" traditional views and beliefs that people who constitute sexual minorities are defective, pathological and/or abominable, i.e., an ideology derived from and reinforced by Western moral and medical models of human development.

The Moral Model

The judgment of abomination is buttressed through application of the moral model, often based on Judeo-Christian biblical interpretation. Though there is surprisingly little said about "homosexuality" in the Bible (no more than eight texts which may or may not refer to it), interpretation of these biblical texts is used to condemn "homosexuals" as evil and diseased or as manifestations of God's displeasure (Helminiak, 1994; McClain, 1993; Swidler, 1993). As the Episcopal Bishop Reverend John S. Spong observed: "In my priestly and Episcopal career I have watched the literal Bible be quoted to justify racial segregation, to ensure continued sexist oppression of women by the Christian church, and to perpetuate a killing homophobia in our corporate life" (Helminiak, 1994, p. 9).

The moral model often provides the structural-cultural ideology for rationalizing the practice of *moral exclusion*, i.e., excluding individuals and/or groups from one's application of doctrines of justice, fairness, and equality (Opotow, 1990). Moral exclusion makes it possible to engage in behavior that is generally outside the scope of what is acceptable to one's values, norms, and beliefs (Opotow, 1990), behavior that often constitutes the very definition of violence. For people who identify, or are perceived as, gay, lesbian, intersexual, bisexual or transgendered, it has resulted in past and current practices of segregation, congregation, invisibility, isolation, discrimination, hatred, violence, and genocide (Blumenfeld, 1992; Feinberg, 1996; Helminiak, 1994; Kirk & Madsen, 1989; MacKenzie, 1994). *Moral exclusion has been a primary mechanism to justify and render invisible the institutional and structural-cultural levels of antigay violence.*

Though Kirk and Madsen (1989) primarily focused on gay males, their work is useful in identifying what the majority of heterosexual people who are not gay affirming think of people who are gay. To a certain extent, these beliefs and practices are used as grounds to justify the moral exclusion of the sexual minority populations, individually and societally. Kirk and Madsen documented how heterosexual people believe that: there aren't many gay people in North America; all gay people are easy to spot (by their names, voices, bodies, demeanors, or careers); gay people are gay by choice and as a result of sin, insanity, and/or seduction; gay people defy the Laws of Nature, i.e., gay = sin; homosexuality is a mental illness; homosexuality is caused by recruitment; gay people are kinky, loathsome sex addicts; gay people are suicidally unhappy because they are gay; and gay people are unproductive and untrustworthy members of society, i.e., the "commie-pinko-faggot" analogy.

These beliefs play into a distorted and universally applied "homosexual lifestyle." To the general public, this lifestyle consists of extreme negative and destructive behaviors and characteristics. Thus, homosexual lifestyle, as well as bisexual and transgendered lifestyle, is portrayed as involving pathological lying (constant concealment); the rejection of morality; narcissism; hedonism; promiscuity; self-indulgence; self-destructiveness; indulgence of private behavior in public; sexual predatoriness; sado-masochistic behavior; sexual polygamy (gay men and bisexual people); hatred of women (gay men); hatred of men (lesbians); indulgence in bars, alcohol, and drugs; coldness; bitchiness; "in-your-face attitudes"; oppressive political correctness; and aggressive nonconformity.

These outdated and unsubstantiated myths and beliefs about sexual minority lifestyle, fueled by "expert" opinions, whispers, smirks, innuendoes and jokes, are often the only reality many people have. Armed with this "reality," family members, friends, and colleagues of people who are gay, lesbian, bisexual, intersexual or transgendered are poorly prepared to make sense out of sexual orientation and sexual identity disclosures. It becomes a slow and painful process to reach the realization that people who are gay, lesbian, bisexual, intersexual, and transgendered are not the problem; the problem is a misinformed society (Griffin, Wirth, & Wirth, 1986).

This lifestyle image is so pervasive that some gay writers accept it as reality, while acknowledging that no research studies exist to support such assertions (see, for example, Bawer, 1994; Kirk & Madsen, 1990). Such writers point out the "shameful gay lifestyle" in order to convince people who are gay and lesbian (discarding those who are bisexual and transgendered) to lead a life beyond reproach, more perfect than heterosexual people. Similar to women and people of color having to work twice as hard to go half as far, people who are gay, lesbian, bisexual or transgendered need to lead twice as clean lives to earn half as much respect. Such messages, repeated often enough, establish unjust social expectations. They also fuel the flame of self-degradation and create an atmosphere of viewing self-destructive acts as "understandable" and to a certain extent acceptable.

Such heterosexist beliefs, constituting structural-cultural levels of anti-gay violence, play out in devalued social roles and negative labeling (Lee,

1994). They combine to socially define and reinforce a negative and pathological "homosexual, bisexual, transgendered lifestyle" image. Labeling a person as a deviant in the community legitimizes isolation from the rest of the society and contributes to the stripping of dignity, civil rights, and personal autonomy, constituting institutional levels of violence (Goffman, 1961). This phenomenon creates devaluation (Condeluci, 1991) and encourages acts of violence at the individual level (Stuab, 1987). Jokes beget harassment begets threats beget violence.

Labeling produces long and lasting stereotypes as well (Biklen & Knoll, 1987). Such labeling and stereotyping promotes negative and inferior expectations at the structural-cultural level for people who are part of sexual minority populations, and a corresponding series of disempowering experiences at the institutional and individual level. Self-concept, identity formation, and self-esteem are adversely impacted (Lee, 1994), triggering intrapersonal violence. The prevalence of negative stereotypes and beliefs also makes it difficult for gay, lesbian, intersexual, bisexual, and transgendered people to form alliances with each other as well as other disempowered groups (Onken, Danis, & Wambach, 1995). It isn't easy to unlearn the structural-cultural myths and beliefs of the "homosexual, bisexual, transgendered lifestyle," but replacing such beliefs with facts frees people to move into the light of a more balanced reality (Griffin, Wirth, & Wirth, 1986).

The Medical Model

In general human services, the medical model has the most influential and embedded structural-cultural roots (Condeluci, 1991). Unfortunately, application of the medical model frequently results in indirect, at times unintentional, antigay violence at the institutional and individual levels through its attempts to "fix" the non-heterosexual.

The medical model, based on the application of science, holds that the person with the "condition" is manifesting physical and/or mental deficits. The "expert" (i.e., the professional) decides how best to restore or fix the person to fit in, i.e., turning the sickness into wellness. The onus for change rests squarely on the shoulders of the patient/client, who needs to change, adapt, or adjust to the existing world (Condeluci, 1991).

The medical model is omnipotent particularly in mental health, which is often subsumed under general health policy (Kiesler, 1992). In Western heterosexually dominated society, homosexuality itself is often still considered a pathological "condition." It wasn't until 1973 that the American Psychiatric Association removed the term "homosexuality" from the official manual that lists all mental and emotional disorders, i.e., the *Diagnostic and Statistical Manual* (Singer & Deschamps, 1994).

Viewing people who are not heterosexual as defective and pathological, however, remains lodged in Western mental health de facto practices. These structural-cultural level images fit well with stereotypes of the emotionally disturbed and/or developmentally incomplete lesbian, gay, bisexual, intersexual or transgendered person, stereotypes that are still prevalent and widely held by practitioners (Brown, 1989; Caldwell, 1993; DeCrescenzo, 1984; Hutchins & Kaahumanu, 1991; Rudolph, 1988; Tievsky, 1988). As psychoanalysis gained popularity in the 1950s, the medical treatment for this condition evolved into having the gay, lesbian or bisexual individual suppress his or her sexual orientation and identity in order to live as or pass as a "normal" heterosexual person, i.e., a heterosexual shift (MacKenzie, 1994; Miller, 1995). This "therapeutic" practice, often called conversion therapy, continues today (Gonsiorek & Weinrich, 1991), even in light of the American Psychological Association's 1990 finding that scientific evidence does not show that conversion therapy works and that it can do more harm than good (Blommer, n.d.). Simply stated, conversion therapy is sanctioned, institutional antigay violence.

Of particular significance is the impact of the medical model and its relationship to the concept of sexual orientation. In the past, both scholarly and scientific efforts to define and understand sexual orientation have been hindered by two assumptions: (a) homosexuality is an indication of psychopathology and (b) sexual orientation is dichotomous, i.e., heterosexual or homosexual (Fox, 1995). Defining and understanding sexual orientation has been further complicated by the frequent interchange of the terms sexual orientation, sexual preference, and homosexual lifestyle. On the structural-cultural level, these assumptions and interchanges combine to convey that sexual orientation is a matter of conscious choice (Blumenfeld & Raymond, 1988). In the public perception, choice and change are closely related.

> The attitudinal belief goes: "If gay persons choose to be gay, then they can choose to not be gay. They can change. They do not have to act on their gay feelings. Therefore, all the forces of the society should be brought to bear on gay and lesbian persons to force them into the straight and narrow path of heterosexuality." (Griffin, Wirth, & Wirth, 1986, p. 34)

The choice/change mind-set sanctions institutional and individual levels of violence in the name of corrective treatment and therapy. It keeps professionals and the general public from: (a) examining their attitudes, beliefs, and behaviors regarding people who are gay, lesbian, bisexual, intersexual or transgendered; (b) from taking steps necessary to change those attitudes, beliefs, and behaviors; and (c) from accepting each individual's right to have a different sexual orientation. When people examine and disregard the choice/change mind-set, their difficulty in accepting such people is greatly eased (Griffin, Wirth, & Wirth, 1986).

The medical model continues to hold harsher and more violent repercussions for transgendered and intersexual people. Transgendered people who cross-dress, cross-gender identify, and/or cross-sex identify remain listed as persons with mental and emotional disorders in the DSM, e.g., gender dysphoria, transvestic fetishism, etc. (MacKenzie, 1994). It is common clinical knowledge that most cross-dressers are heterosexual (Docter, 1988; King, 1993). The definition of transvestic fetishism, within its own diagnostic criteria, acknowledges that the person is heterosexual. But cross-dressers apparently are not heterosexual enough, as their treatment becomes that of suppressing the cross-dressing behavior. Such behavior constitutes sanctioned, institutional levels of violence through alienation, depriving people of their own sense of who they are.

For individuals labeled as transsexuals, treatment has become one of sex reassignment surgery (Docter, 1988; Feinberg, 1996; MacKenzie, 1994). This practice is increasingly being called into question by a growing number of people in the transgendered movement, who seek the freedom to live the gender of their inclination without being subjected to the sanctioned, institutional violence of genitalia mutilation in the name of corrective treatment (Feinberg, 1996; MacKenzie, 1994).

The phenomenon of intersexuality is essentially suppressed, withheld from the general public (Nagle, 1995). When a recognizable intersexual infant is born, the physician surgically and hormonally manipulates the infant into an assigned sex, though such action is not medically necessary to maintain the physical health of the infant (Feinberg, 1996). Such alterations occur sometimes with and sometimes without the parents' consent or knowledge (Nagle, 1995). If the secondary sex characteristics of the assigned sex fail to appear at puberty, these children are treated with hormones to facilitate the development of secondary sex characteristics to match the initial sex assignment, regardless of the genetic makeup, anatomy, and endocrine status of the child (Wishik & Pierce, 1995).

An increasing number of adult intersexual people, however, are challenging their medical treatment, their lack of consent to such treatment, and the deeply held beliefs that continue to justify such treatment. They point out that such beliefs constitute a structural-cultural ideology that sanctions institutional violence through surgical and hormonal manipulation in the name of corrective treatment. The Intersex Society of North America advances a model for the management of intersexual children that "is based upon avoidance of harmful or unnecessary surgery, qualified professional mental health care for the intersexual child and his/her family, and empowering the intersexual person to understand his/her own status and to choose (or reject) any medical intervention" (n.d.).

Stigma

Both the moral model and the medical model establish a structural-cultural antigay environment in which people who are gay, lesbian, bisexual, intersexual or transgendered are stigmatized for not conforming to heterosexual standards. Stigmatizing involves the process of marking or labeling someone as possessing a *stigma,* an attribute that is deeply discrediting–so much so that people believe that the person with the stigma is not quite human (Goffman, 1963). As Goffman (1963) observes, to stigmatize is to trigger a self-fulfilling mind-set. On the assumption that they are not quite human, people and societies exercise varieties of discrimination, through which they effectively, if often unthinkingly, reduce the life chances of the people who are stigmatized.

People and societies construct a stigma-theory, a structural-cultural ideology to explain the inferiority of the people who are stigmatized and account for the danger they represent, sometimes rationalizing an animosity based on other differences. People and societies tend to impute a wide range of imperfections on the basis of the original one. Further, they may perceive their defensive responses as directly caused by the defects of the people who are stigmatized. Both the defects of the people who are stigmatized and the destructive and degrading responses towards them are viewed as justifiable and just retribution.

In essence, the process of stigmatization is structural-cultural violence in action and provides further justification for moral exclusion. The moral model reinforces the structural-cultural belief that not being heterosexual is sinful, immoral and an abomination. The medical model reinforces the structural-cultural belief of homosexuality, bisexuality, intersexuality and transgenderedness as mental illnesses or at least stymied, interrupted and incomplete personal and sexual development. Both provide a structural-cultural rationale for believing that people who are gay, lesbian, bisexual, intersexual or transgendered are "not quite human" or at least not complete humans and thus can be "justifiably" excluded from application of doctrines of justice, fairness, and equality. Thus, the structural-cultural foundation is laid for antigay violence, serving to sanction, or at least permit, institutional and individual levels of antigay violence.

GENDER OPPRESSION

This structural-cultural foundation for antigay violence is further enforced by the impact of gender socialization. Gender is the social construct applied to biological sex, "the dual category system in which certain human traits are assigned to one biological sex and certain traits to the other" (Baker, 1992, p. 257). North American traditional views regarding gender, gender roles, and gender socialization feed the discomfort, fear, and hatred of sexual minority people, as well as interrelated subjugation and violence directed at women, i.e., sexism.

The gender attributions people give themselves and are given by others color all aspects of psychological, social, political, and economic exchange. Gender is "one of the most effective means of social control. From birth we are enculturated into a dual gender system, reinforced by all the major institutions" (MacKenzie, 1994, p. 1). There is no real non-stigmatized or non-sensationalized category for those who are both and neither. As Feinberg observes

> How can I tell you about their [transgendered people's] battle when the words *woman* and *man, feminine* and *masculine*, are almost the only words that exist in the English language to describe all the vicissitudes of bodies and styles of expression? . . . There were no words that we'd go out of our way to use that made us feel good about ourselves. (1996, p. ix)

In contemporary Western cultures, gender includes the structural-cultural judgment that it is right and natural to: (a) divide people into two and only two mutually exclusive biological sexes (i.e., *genderism*), (b) require compulsory monosexuality, i.e., sexual orientation toward one and only one of the two recognized biological sexes (*monosexism*), and (c) define "real" men and women as only those who are heterosexual (*heterosexism*) (Nagle, 1995; Wishik & Pierce, 1995). Genderism, monosexism, and heterosexism combine to form a powerful structural-cultural ideology that undergirds the stigmatization and moral exclusion of people who are gay, lesbian, bisexual, intersexual, and transgendered and gives rise to and sanctions the expression of anti-gay violence.

This structural-cultural ideology is further sanctioned and reinforced by traditional notions of gender, that is, what constitutes a healthy, normal man or woman. In Western culture, maleness and masculinity are seen as a positive force, as a presence, and as primary; femaleness and femininity are seen as a negative force, an absence, and as a derivative and thus inherently flawed and lacking (Devor, 1989). In essence, gender is constructed out of a structural-cultural ideology that is anti-woman and gives rise to violence directed at women. The negative and self-degrading effects upon women of the myth that the male is normative has been widespread and undeniable (Long, 1990; Pugliesi, 1989; Sanford & Donovan, 1984) and constitutes violence turned inward, i.e., the intrapersonal dimension of violence.

This way of seeing serves to promote the domination of males over females and the reinforcement of male power, i.e., a patriarchal hierarchy (Blumenfeld & Raymond, 1988). In Western society the dominant bipolar gender ideology incorporates and reinforces this patriarchy, specifically White patriarchy.[5] This patriarchal schema and its assumptions underlie the psychological, social, economic, and political components of gender (Devor, 1989). Thus, gender socialization and patriarchal hierarchy are intricately linked, providing a structural-cultural ideology of sexism and the institutionalized oppression of women. Even within the gay community, this patriarchal hierarchy and sexism exists (Marcus, 1993).

This oppression of women is kept in place by an ideology of superiority and privilege based on being male. Misogyny, the hatred of women, further stigmatizes females for being female (Devor, 1989). These provide the structural-cultural roots and justification for use of institutional and individual levels of anti-female violence. Women learn that being female means being subjected to sexual victimization at the hands of men. Women have little right to psychic privacy in public places and are vulnerable to sexual assault at any time (Devor, 1989). Sexual victimization and assault are examples of individual violence directed at women and only constitute the visible violence directed at women. Institutional violence, for example widespread exclusion of female participants in research studies, is often invisible but more prevalent (Van Soest & Bryant, 1995).

Thus within Western society, heterosexual but feminine males are stigmatized as failed men and heterosexual but masculine females are stigmatized both as females and as failed women (Devor, 1989). Out, self-identified gay males (as well as those assumed to be) are stigmatized as failed men as well as failed heterosexuals, with bisexual and transgendered males also contending with failed monosexuality. Out, self-identified lesbians (as well as those assumed to be) are stigmatized as females, failed women, and failed heterosexuals, with bisexual and transgendered females also contending with failed monosexuality. Even within the gay and lesbian communities, people who identify as bisexual or transgendered, people who openly cross-dress, men who are too "swishy," and women who are too "butch," are subject to stigmatization.

Individual and institutional harassment, discrimination, and violence accompany each stigmatization accomplished at the structural-cultural level. Each stigma feeds and interacts with other stigmas that may be heaped onto a person or group, exponentially increasing the resulting harassment, discrimination, and violence, as well as the difficulty in managing and undoing the impact of the stigmas.

Sexism, genderism, heterosexism, monosexism, patriarchal hierarchy-all of these, when combined with power, are forms of gender oppression. All of these feed into and reinforce the structural-cultural level of anti-gay and anti-female violence. There are no permanent institutionalized roles or safe spaces for individuals who live outside of the dominant patriarchal heterosexual bipolar gender world (MacKenzie, 1994).

CONCLUSION

Prejudice, discrimination, and loathing of sexual minorities are condoned in North American society. Sexism, genderism, heterosexism, monosexism, and patriarchal hierarchy are social diseases of domination with the enculturation so pervasive that no individual is immune (Sunfrog, 1995). Persons who are gay, lesbian, intersexual, bisexual, or transgendered have grown up in homes without parental or societal role models who share these orientations and identities. Their parents, families, friends, and communities often adopt the values and attitudes of the mainstream, becoming environments perpetuating patriarchal, heterosexist, genderist, and sexist myths and stereotypes (Kirk & Madsen, 1989; MacKenzie, 1994).

Out of fear, many people who are gay, lesbian, intersexual, bisexual, or transgendered remain in hiding, their "condition" closeted from all but a trusted few (MacKenzie, 1994; Wishik & Pierce, 1995). Intrapersonal violence in the form of self-degradation, shame, self-doubt and suicide can result (Garnets & Kimmel, 1993; Proctor & Groze, 1994). Not complying with gender and sexuality norms and the moral and medical model modes of treatment (i.e., suppression, aversion and conversion therapy, and sex reassignment surgery) has resulted in past (and current) institutional violent practices of invisibility, isolation, hospitalization, imprisonment, marginalization, rejection, discrimination, harassment, assault, and death (De-Cecco, 1985; Kirk & Madsen, 1989; MacKenzie, 1994). Being open about sexual identities has resulted in such individual acts of violence as name-calling, verbal harassment, physical harassment, physical beatings, and murder.

All of these practices constitute direct and indirect violent acts of omission, repression, and alienation that result in harm on an intrapersonal, interpersonal, and collective level for people who constitute sexual minority populations. In the US, all such violence has been sanctioned by a structural-cultural belief system passing judgment on what constitutes morality and normality using doctrines of white, male, heterosexual superiority.

Much human potential is squashed and wasted in people who live for years in secret self-hatred, taught to be afraid of their own hearts, and in the lives of their companions, friends and family, who fail to recognize, share and nurture this love. The first step for all individuals in the fight against such internalized oppression and violence (regardless of sex, gender, sexual orientation, or culture) is to find the embedded seeds of heterosexism, sexism, and genderism in their consciousness and to confront them. Authentic freedom from sex, gender, and sexual orientation inequality is also freedom from the tenets of authority, coercion, violence, and power that define many affectional-sexual relationships (Sunfrog, 1995).

This freedom, in turn, can become the fuel to feed the fight against the tenets of authority, coercion, violence, and power that define many social-political relationships. That sexual minorities have survived, and at times persevered, is a testament to their resilience and varied and multiple strengths. In recent years, these groups have increased their visibility; developed individual and community identities, pride and cultures; and fought for their human and civil rights and for an end to antigay violence (MacKenzie, 1994; Marcus, 1992; Tucker, 1995). It has been and continues to be a long and difficult struggle. But it is a struggle that celebrates a love that is worth fighting for, and ultimately it is a struggle that must succeed.

NOTES

1. For the purposes of this article *antigay* is defined as inclusively applying to the sexual minority populations, i.e., anti-gay, anti-lesbian, anti-bisexual, anti-intersexual, and anti-transgendered.

2. The sexual minority population does not include extreme patterns of sexual desire or interpersonal behavior that are linked to imbalances of power (such as pedophilia, the desire for adult sexual contact with young children) and acts of violence. It is important to acknowledge, however, that what constitutes pathology and normality in sexual desire and behavior is a culturally determined one.

What is acceptable (e.g., Danish same sex unions) or even sacred (e.g., Melanesian male to male puberty ceremonies) in one culture is not in others (Blumenfeld & Raymond, 1988).

3. *Intersexuality* means possessing the congenital intermingling of male and female sexual and/or reproductive organs, in other words, having (in varying degrees) both male and female genetic, anatomic, and hormonal properties (Feinberg, 1996; Nagle, 1995). Intersexual individuals are born with these physical attributions.

4. Transgendered people traverse, bridge, or blur the boundary of the *gender expression* (boy/man/masculinity, girl/woman/femininity) they were assigned at birth. The term is used inclusively, and encompasses trans*sexual* men and women who also traverse the boundary of the *sex* (male or female) they were assigned at birth. Some transgendered people choose surgery or hormones as a part of this process; most do not (Feinberg, 1996). Many individuals in the gender community prefer the terms cross-dresser, cross-gender identified and/or transgenderedist, which are less stigmatizing than medically derived terms.

5. Though beyond the scope of this article, see Van Soest and Bryant (1995) for an excellent discussion of the impact of racism in understanding violence.

REFERENCES

Aaron, L. (1995). *Prayers for Bobby*. New York: HarperCollins.
Baker, K. (1992). Bisexual feminist politics: Because bisexuality is not enough. In E.R. Weise (Ed.), *Closer to home: Bisexuality & feminism* (pp. 255-267). Seattle: Seal Press.
Barber, K., & Holmes, S. (Eds.). (1994). *Testimonies: A collection of lesbian coming out stories*. Boston, MA: Alyson Publications.
Bawer, B. (1994). *A place at the table: The gay individual in American society*. Poseidon Press.
Biklen, D., & Knoll, J. (1987). The disabled minority. In S. Taylor, D. Biklen & J. Knoll (Eds.), *Community integration for people with severe disabilities* (pp. 3-24). New York: Teachers College Press.
Blommer, D.J. (n.d.). *Psychology and you: Answers to your questions about sexual orientation and homosexuality*. Washington, DC: American Psychological Association.
Blumenfeld, W.J. (Ed.). (1992). *Homophobia: How we all pay the price*. Boston: Beacon Press.
Blumenfeld, W.J., & Raymond, D. (1988). *Looking at gay and lesbian life*. Boston: Beacon Press.
Brown, L.S. (1989). New voices, new visions: Toward a lesbian/gay paradigm for psychology. *Psychology of Women Quarterly, 13*, 445-458.
Bulhan, H.A. (1985). *Frantz Fanon and the psychology of oppression*. New York: Plenum Press.

Caldwell, S. (1993). Gay men and HIV: The band plays on. In V. Lynch, G. Lloyd, & M. Fimbres (Eds.), *The changing face of AIDS: Implications for social work practice* (pp. 152-172). Westport, CT: Auburn House.

Clark, K. (1996, March 21). El Paso reports nation's sharpest increase in anti-gay violence. *The Texas Triangle, 4*(23).

Condeluci, A. (1991). *Interdependence: The route to community.* Winter Park, FL: PMD Publishers Group, Inc.

DeCecco, J.P. (Ed.). (1985). *Bashers, baiters & bigots: Homophobia in American society.* New York: Harrington Park Press.

DeCrescenzo, T.S. (1984). Homophobia: A study of the attitudes of mental health professionals toward homosexuality. In R. Schoenberg, R.S. Goldberg, & D.A. Shore (Eds.), *Homosexuality and social work* (pp. 115-135). New York: The Haworth Press, Inc.

Devor, H. (1989). *Gender blending: Confronting the limits of duality.* Bloomington: Indiana University Press.

Dew, R.F. (1994). *The family heart: A memoir of when our son came out.* New York: Ballantine Books.

Docter, R.F. (1988). *Transvestites and transsexuals: Toward a theory of cross-gender behavior.* New York: Plenum Press.

Feinberg, L. (1996). *Transgendered warriors: Making history from Joan of Arc to RuPaul.* Boston: Beacon Press.

Fellows, W. (1996). *Farm boys: Lives of gay men from the rural midwest.* Madison, WI: The University of Wisconsin Press.

Fox, R.C. (1995). Bisexual identities. In A.R. D'Augelli & C.J. Patterson (Eds.), *Lesbian, gay, and bisexual identities over the lifespan: Psychological perspectives* (pp. 48-86). New York: Oxford University Press.

Gallagher, J. (1995, July 11). Hate crime: Special report. *The Advocate, 685,* 30-37.

Garnets, L.D., & Kimmel, D.C. (Eds.). (1993). *Psychological perspectives on lesbian & gay male experiences.* New York: Columbia University Press.

Goffman, E. (1961). *Asylums: Essays on the social situation of mental patients and other inmates.* Garden City, NY: Doubleday & Co.

Goffman, E. (1963). *Stigma: Notes on the management of spoiled identity.* Englewood Cliffs, NJ: Prentice-Hall, Inc.

Gonsiorek, J.C., & Weinrich, J.D. (Eds.). (1991). *Homosexuality: Research implications for public policy.* Newbury Park, CA: Sage.

Griffin, C., Wirth, M., & Wirth, A. (1986). *Beyond acceptance.* Englewood Cliffs, NJ: Prentice-Hall.

Helminiak, D.A. (1994). *What the Bible really says about homosexuality.* San Francisco: Alamo Square Press.

Herek, G.M. (1993). The context of anti-gay violence: Notes on cultural and psychological heterosexism. In R. Cleaver & P. Myers (Eds.), *A certain terror: Heterosexism, militarism, violence, & change* (pp. 221-233). Chicago: American Friends Service Committee.

Hutchins, L., & Kaahumanu, L. (Eds.). (1991). *Bi any other name: Bisexual people speak out*. Boston: Alyson Publications.

Intersex Society of North America. (n.d.) *What is intersexuality?* San Francisco.

Kiesler, C.A. (1992). U.S. mental health policy: Doomed to fail. *American Psychologist, 47*(9), 1077-1082.

King, D. (1993). *The transvestite and the transsexual*. Brookfield, VT: Ashgate Publishing Company.

Kirk, M. & Madsen, H. (1989). *After the ball: How America will conquer its fear & hatred of gays in the 90's*. New York: Plume, a Division of Penguin Books USA, Inc.

Lee, J.A.B. (1994). *The empowerment approach to social work practice*. New York: Columbia University Press.

Long, V. (1990). Masculinity, femininity, and women scientists' self-esteem and self-acceptance. *The Journal of Psychology, 125*(3), 263-270.

Louganis, G. (1995). *Breaking the surface*. New York: Random House.

MacKenzie, G.O. (1994). *Transgendered nation*. Bowling Green, OH: Bowling Green University Popular Press.

Maguen, S. (1993). Teen suicide: The government's cover-up and America's lost children. In R. Cleaver & P. Myers (Eds.), *A certain terror: Heterosexism, militarism, violence & change* (pp. 239-249). Chicago: American Friends Service Committee.

Marcus, E. (1992). *Making history: The struggle for gay and lesbian equal rights, 1945-1990*. New York: HarperCollins.

Marcus, E. (1993). *Is it a choice? Answers to 300 of the most frequently asked questions about gays and lesbians*. San Francisco: Harper Collins.

McClain, G.D. (Ed.). (1993). *Social questions bulletin, Jan.-Feb.* Staten Island, NY: Methodist Federation for Social Action.

Miller, N. (1989). *In search of gay America*. New York: Harper & Row.

Miller, N. (1995). *Out of the past: Gay and lesbian history from 1869 to the present*. New York: Vintage Books.

Monette, P. (1992). *Becoming a man: Half a life story*. New York: HarperCollins Publishers.

Nagle, J. (1995). Framing radical bisexuality: Toward a gender agenda. In N. Tucker (Ed.), *Bisexual politics: Theories, queries, and visions* (pp. 305-314). New York: The Haworth Press, Inc.

Onken, S.J., Danis, F.S., & Wambach, K.G. (1995). *Oppression, cultural competency, and empowerment: Foundations for lesbian and gay content*. Paper presented at the Annual Program Meeting, Council on Social Work Education, San Diego, CA.

Opotow, S. (1990). Moral exclusion and injustice: An introduction. *Journal of Social Issues, 46*(1), 1-20.

Penelope, J. & Wolfe, S.J. (Eds.). (1989). *The original coming out stories*. Freedom, CA: The Crossing Press.

Proctor, C.D., & Groze, V.K. (1994). Risk factors for suicide among gay, lesbian, and bisexual youths. *Social Work, 39*(5), 504-513.

Pugliesi, K. (1989). Social support and self-esteem as intervening variables in the relationship between social roles and women's well-being. *Community Mental Health Journal, 25*(2), 87-100.

Rudolph, J. (1988). Counselors' attitudes toward homosexuality: A selective review of the literature. *Journal of Counseling and Development, 67,* 165-168.

Saks, A., & Curtis, W. (Eds.). (1994). *Revelations: A collection of gay male coming out stories.* Boston, MA: Alyson Publications.

Salmi, J. (1993). *Violence and democratic society.* London: Zed Books.

Sanford, L., & Donovan, M. (1984). *Women and self-esteem* (1st Ed.). New York: Anchor Press.

Sears, J.T. (1991). *Growing up gay in the South: Race, gender, and journeys of the spirit.* Binghamton, NY: Harrington Park Press.

Singer, B.L., & Deschamps, D. (Eds.). (1994). *Gay & lesbian stats.* New York: The New Press.

Stuab, E. (1987). *Moral exclusion and extreme destructiveness: Personal goal theory, differential evaluation, moral equilibration and steps along the continuum of destruction.* Paper presented at the American Psychological Association, NY.

Sunfrog. (1995). Pansies against patriarchy: Gender blur, bisexual men, and queer liberation. In N. Tucker (Ed.), *Bisexual politics: Theories, queries, and visions* (pp. 319-324). New York: The Haworth Press, Inc.

Swidler, A. (Ed.). (1993). *Homosexuality and world religions.* Valley Forge, PA: Trinity Press International.

Tievsky, D.L. (1988). Homosexual clients and homophobic social workers. *Journal of Independent Social Work, 2*(3), 51-62.

Tucker, N. (Ed.). (1995). *Bisexual politics: Theories, queries, and visions.* New York: The Haworth Press, Inc.

Van Soest, D., & Bryant, S. (1995). Violence reconceptualized for social work: The urban dilemma. *Social Work, 40*(4), 549-557.

Wishik, H., & Pierce, C. (1995). *Sexual orientation and identity: Heterosexual, lesbian, gay, and bisexual journeys.* Laconia, NH: New Dynamics Publications.

Hate Crimes Motivated by Sexual Orientation: Police Reporting and Training

Lacey M. Sloan
Linda King
Sandra Sheppard

SUMMARY. The enactment of hate crimes legislation raised awareness of the severity of crimes motivated by animus toward individuals and communities. This national telephone survey found that states which mandate local law enforcement agencies to report hate crimes generally have high compliance rates; states without mandatory reporting requirements have few law enforcement agencies that report these crimes. Law enforcement training on hate crime varies from state to state, with few states including information specifically addressing hate crimes motivated by sexual orientation. *[Article copies available for a fee from The Haworth Document Delivery Service: 1-800-342-9678. E-mail address: getinfo@haworthpressinc.com]*

Growing awareness in this country of crimes motivated by bias and hatred of minority groups resulted in the passage of the Hate Crimes Statistics Act of 1990. Since then, the FBI has collected information on

Lacey M. Sloan, PhD, is Assistant Professor, Graduate School of Social Work, University of Houston, Houston, TX 77204. Linda King, MSW, doctoral candidate, and Sandra Sheppard, MSSW, are both affiliated with SUNY-Buffalo, 359 Baldy Hall, Buffalo, NY 14260.

[Haworth co-indexing entry note]: "Hate Crimes Motivated by Sexual Orientation: Police Reporting and Training." Sloan, Lacey M., Linda King, and Sandra Sheppard. Co-published simultaneously in *Journal of Gay & Lesbian Social Services* (The Haworth Press, Inc.) Vol. 8, No. 3, 1998, pp. 25-39; and: *Violence and Social Injustice Against Lesbian, Gay and Bisexual People* (ed: Lacey M. Sloan, and Nora S. Gustavsson) The Haworth Press, Inc., 1998, pp. 25-39. Single or multiple copies of this article are available for a fee from The Haworth Document Delivery Service [1-800-342-9678, 9:00 a.m. - 5:00 p.m. (EST). E-mail address: getinfo@haworthpressinc.com].

incidents of hate crimes and published annual reports. Although several organizations and authors have undertaken research to quantify (Berrill, 1990; Comstock, 1991; National Gay and Lesbian Task Force, 1993) and describe (Herek & Berrill, 1992) hate crimes against lesbians, gay men, and bisexuals, this has yet to be fully accomplished. Heterosexism, homophobia, and the invisibility of lesbians, gay men, and bisexuals makes underreporting of hate crimes motivated by sexual orientation an ongoing problem. Reports by activists in the gay community of improper or half-hearted implementation of Federal hate crime legislation, and the disparities between Federal Uniform Crime Report (UCR) statistics and those collected by gay advocacy organizations, raise concern regarding the consistency of law enforcement training and underscore the problem. This research examines law enforcement reporting and training on hate crimes motivated by sexual orientation, and recommends ways that social workers and activists can assist in the development and delivery of specialized training to law enforcement officers.

Hate crimes affect the entire U.S. population and one only need open up a newspaper to read evidence of violence fueled by bias and hate in rural, suburban, and urban communities alike. The immediate victims of hate crime motivated by bias against a particular sexual orientation include the gay, lesbian, bisexual, or transgendered individuals who experience the violence. Individuals who appear to the perpetrator to be gay may also experience victimization similar to that experienced by openly gay and lesbian individuals (Saraceno, 1993). Secondary victims include the greater gay and lesbian community, which begins to live in fear of unexpected and unwarranted attacks in a variety of forms. Beyond the immediate gay and lesbian community, individuals in the greater community witness the attacks and may come to believe that soon they themselves will become targets by virtue of characteristics that make them unique or those they may share with the target group (Lawrence, 1994; Kibelstis, 1995; Mason, 1993).

During 1994, hate crimes motivated by sexual orientation bias accounted for 12% of the 5,932 hate crime incidents reported to the Federal Bureau of Investigation (FBI) by state-level uniform crime reporting units (U.S. Department of Justice, 1994). Sexual orientation bias matched racial bias in motivating the highest number of murders (3% of the total reported murders); and accounted for 7% of aggravated assault; 7% of simple assault; 10% of intimidation; and 100% of all incidents classified as "other" (U.S. Department of Justice, 1994). In 1990, only 2,771 of over 16,000 participating law enforcement agencies reported Federal hate-related crimes to the FBI, suggesting a trend of severe underreporting; state statistics, if collected, are even less reliable (Herek & Berrill, 1992; Kibelstis, 1995; *Harvard Law Review*, 1993; Saraceno, 1993).

Recognizing sexual orientation bias as a punishable motivation for hate crime should have had a perceptible impact on the development of training programs for law enforcement officers as the first responders to these crimes. Nationwide training seminars teach law enforcement personnel how to investigate and report hate crimes (U.S. Department of Justice, 1994) but few training programs offer specialized training modules that respond to a concern that "[s]ome law enforcement personnel regard crimes against gays and lesbians as less serious than those hate crimes related to ethnicity/national origin" (National Organization of Black Law Enforcement Officers, 1991, p. 15). This study analyzed the methods and means used by law enforcement to report hate crimes motivated by sexual orientation bias, and the training used to educate and sensitize law enforcement officers to these crimes.

THEORETICAL BASES OF HATE CRIMES

Frederick Lawrence, Professor of Law at Boston University, described two models to understand and analyze hate crime: the "discriminatory selection model" and the "racial animus model" (1994). The discriminatory selection model defines criminality based on the perpetrator's choice of victim on the basis of victim characteristics, such as race or sexual orientation (Lawrence, 1994). This model acknowledges and punishes the discriminatory selection of a victim but is not concerned with the motivation for choosing a particular category of victim[1] (Lawrence, 1994). The racial animus model "defines these crimes on the basis of the perpetrator's animus toward the . . . group of the victim and the centrality of this animus in the perpetrator's motivation for committing the crime" (Lawrence, 1994, p. 376). In other words, the animus model acknowledges the malevolent intent of the perpetrator, not just the discriminatory selection of a victim[2] (Lawrence, 1994). All animus crimes would, by their very nature, also be considered discriminatory, but the reverse is not true (Lawrence, 1994). Laws based on the discriminatory model include crimes that, although biased, are not motivated by hate or animosity towards any group (Lawrence, 1994).

The federal hate crimes reporting law, the FBI, and several states are clearly aligned with the animus model but, due to the wording of state statutes, many states cannot be clearly identified as aligning with either model (Lawrence, 1994). Statutes which indicate that a hate crime is committed if a victim is selected on the *basis of* race (or some other protected category) reflect the discriminatory model; statutes which indicate that a hate crime is committed if the victim is selected on the basis of *bias against* the person's race (or other protected category) reflect the animus model. Only Connecticut, Maryland, Pennsylvania, Florida, and New Hampshire specify the element of animus (or hatred) in their statutes (Lawrence, 1994).

Victims and targeted communities expect law enforcement officers to have and exhibit an understanding of the impact of sexual orientation bias crime (Herek, 1989; Jenness, 1995). This includes not only intervening in a crisis and assisting a victim or victims, but also developing a trusting relationship with the gay and lesbian community, implementing preventive measures and providing additional protection, i.e., police-gay/lesbian liaisons, foot patrols, and special task forces (Mason, 1993). Without training that specifically addresses animus and the impact of the crime on the specific victim, target group, and community at large, law enforcement response to crimes motivated by sexual orientation bias will be less effective. The absence of specialized training components suggests a position of neutrality that may be "incorrectly interpreted as anti-gay" (Herek & Berrill, 1992, p. 140).

Hate Crimes Legislation and Reporting

The Hate Crimes Statistics Act of 1990 required the Attorney General to develop a system to collect data from its more than 16,000 voluntary law enforcement agency participants (U.S. Department of Justice, 1994). The Attorney General delegated this responsibility to the FBI; the FBI has incorporated hate crimes as an adjunct to the national Uniform Crime Reports (UCR) program (U.S. Department of Justice, date unknown a). The FBI hate crimes reporting form has a box that can be checked if no hate crimes occurred during the reporting period (referred to as "zero reporting"). However, states are not required to participate in data collection and this has resulted in fewer than 50% of law enforcement agencies providing hate crimes reports to the FBI (U.S. Department of Justice, 1994). Although there has been an increase in the collection and publication of statistical information regarding crimes motivated by sexual orientation bias, activists report that law enforcement investigators continue to rely on traumatized victims and witnesses to report hate motivation rather than on thorough examination of the perpetrator and crime scene for indicators of bias motivations (Jenness, 1995).

The FBI is implementing a new data collection strategy to replace summary based quarterly reports with individual incident reports (National Incident-Based Reporting System [NIBRS]) (U.S. Department of Justice, date unknown b). The NIBRS report allows for much more detailed data collection about victims, perpetrators, and offenses (U.S. Department of Justice, date unknown b). For example, the NIBRS form includes information on type of crime (murder, rape, etc.); location of the crime (bus, store, etc.); bias motivation, including racial, ethnic, religious and sexual orientation; victim type (individual, organization, etc.); number of offenders; and, offender's race. Law enforcement not participating in NIBRS continue to complete quarterly reports which only include a tally of the number of hate crimes which were reported in each quarter.

Following the passage of federal legislation, several states have adopted hate crimes laws which include statutes prohibiting intimidation or interference with civil rights, statutes that create separate bias-motivation crimes, and penalty enhancement provisions (Freeman & Kaminer, 1994). A recent survey of state civil rights laws revealed that 20 states include the phrase "sexual orientation" in the wording of hate crime data collection law; 16 of those 20 states include sexual orientation in hate crimes penalty law; and one of the 16 states, Texas, has hate crimes penalty law that cannot be enforced due to vague wording (Kibelstis, 1995; National Gay and Lesbian Task Force, 1996). At least seven states include training specifications in their general legislation (Freeman & Kaminer, 1994). Indiana's legislature

> dropped sexual orientation from its proposed hate crimes bill . . . [to] encourage support for the measure in the Indiana Senate . . . Texas' hate inclusion of sexual orientation as a protected category almost doomed the statute's passage . . . repeated efforts to pass hate crime laws in Arizona and New York failed because . . . of the inclusion of sexual orientation as a protected category. (Kibelstis, 1995, p. 333-334)

These positions conflict with the intent of the FBI to utilize hate crimes legislation and law enforcement education as "another important tool to confront violent bigotry against individuals on the basis of their . . . sexual orientation . . . " (Freeman & Kaminer, 1994, p. 24).

Nine states have moved beyond penalty enhancement and have civil rights laws that include sexual orientation passed by the legislature (National Gay and Lesbian Task Force, 1995). Several states (15, plus the District of Columbia, out of 41 states with hate crimes laws, specifically include sexual orientation as a protected class under hate crimes laws) formulate definitions of bias crime, and extend existing criminal definitions and statutes (for crimes including vandalism and assault) in an effort to respond effectively to the unique qualities inherent in bias crimes (Jenness, 1995; Kibelstis, 1995; Lawrence, 1994). Homophobia and heterosexism often prevent the extension of protection against bias based on sexual orientation (Kibelstis, 1995).

Law Enforcement Training

Bias or hate crime training programs for law enforcement officers became necessary because these women and men are usually the first service providers to respond to incidences of hate violence, and because they bear the significant responsibility for gathering information that will lead to appropriate legal action. Federal UCR officers have conducted trainings for law enforcement officers from over 1,000 agencies representing all 50 states and the District of Columbia. This training included information on documenting specific information regarding criminal activity when evidence suggests bias or hate motivation (U.S. Department of Justice, 1995). Trainings have also been conducted for state UCR officers so that these persons could train others in their states. However, few states have enacted legislation requiring minimum standards for training in how to approach, evaluate, and assess a crime scene, the victim, and the perpetrator for evidence that may not be obvious or willingly divulged. This lack of training may, in part, account for the underreporting of hate-motivated violence against gays and lesbians (Jenness, 1995; Kibelstis, 1995).

Developing specialized training components that teach law officers to respond competently to sexual orientation bias crime, addresses the belief that

> [b]ias crimes are distinct from parallel crimes. . . . The victim . . . is not attacked for a random reason . . . nor is he attacked for an impersonal reason. . . . Moreover, the . . . victim cannot reasonably minimize the risks of future attacks because he is unable to change the characteristics that make him a victim. (Lawrence, 1994, p. 342)

The development of these training components will convey to officers, victims, perpetrators, and the community at large the particular significance of sexual orientation bias crime as more than merely a gay problem (Jenness, 1995).

Despite the fact that officers respond to an ever-increasing number of bias-motivated violence, the minority of law enforcement receive special training on hate crimes. This training, provided by in house trainers, usually merely extends the existing multiculturalism modules. Very few training programs utilize leaders from the gay and lesbian communities, or advocacy agencies to provide part or all of the training, even though lesbian and gay advocates may be best qualified to provide this training

(Mason, 1993). At the same time, violence motivated by sexual orientation bias represents increasingly "frequent, visible, violent, and culturally legitimated" behaviors (Jenness, 1995, p. 149) that include everything from intimidation to murder (Hate Crimes Statistics, 1994; Herek, 1989; Jenness, 1995; Saraceno, 1993).

Most training modules respond to hate crimes simply by reviewing the actual crime reporting form (either the FBI standard or the accepted form for that state), which has been expanded to include a section of boxes to be checked if the officer observes evidence of sexual orientation bias. Other training modules respond to crimes motivated by sexual orientation bias by extending the component that presents multicultural issues and discrimination. In only rare exceptions do training components specifically address animus, distinctness of bias crimes, and the impact of bias crimes on the victim and society (Lawrence, 1994). Unlike specialized training modules on bias crimes, training that does not include information on animus and the impact of hate crimes fails to adequately teach law enforcement officers the differences between hate crimes and other crimes (Lawrence, 1994).

Community-based organizations have lead the way in designing local interventions for crisis, short-term professional counseling, peer counseling, and group counseling. They provide information about personal control and options, and reinforce the importance of basic human rights. They have initiated a social transformation by focusing their interventions on violence and victimization (Herek, 1990). To some extent, law enforcement providers have responded by acknowledging their responsibility to become accountable for providing culturally competent education, and publishing documentation that reflects, rather than refutes, data collected by a variety of advocacy groups. However, training materials continue to reflect the use of multi-cultural issues, or racism, as catch-all components rather than specializing training components to reflect the specific needs of gay and lesbian bias crime victims in terms of police advocacy (precinct accompaniment, local police liaison, liaison with specialized units), and advocacy with prosecutors (court accompaniment) (Werthheimer, 1992).

RESEARCH METHODS

This research was conducted in four phases: (1) a telephone survey of Uniform Crime Reporting (UCR) officers in 44 of the 50 states in the United States; (2) a telephone survey of persons responsible for training law enforcement recruits and officers in each state; (3) a telephone survey of agencies identified in the literature as having model hate crimes training programs; and (4) a content analysis of the training materials and minimum training standards. Specifically, researchers were interested in determining (1) how hate crimes were reported; (2) how police officers were trained on hate crimes; and (3) what, if anything, was addressed in training about hate crimes against lesbian, gay, bisexual and transgendered persons (LGBT).

For the first phase of this research, persons with primary responsibility for the Uniform Crime Report (UCR) were interviewed, by telephone, for this research (all states except Indiana, Mississippi, Missouri, New Mexico, Ohio and Tennessee–we attempted but were unsuccessful in reaching appropriate persons in these six states). Each UCR officer was interviewed about the methods and forms used to collect data on hate crimes against LGBT. Of specific interest was whether local law enforcement agencies were mandated to report hate crimes and whether zero reporting was mandatory. If a state was utilizing a reporting form that differed from the FBI reporting form, they were asked to send a copy of the form to the researcher.

For the second phase of this research, thirty-eight training officers and training standards officers were interviewed by telephone. Training personnel were interviewed about the curriculum utilized to train recruits and officers (i.e., name of program, type, size, length, components). States which had decentralized training were asked information about minimum training requirements. Training officers were also asked if they thought a model training program existed in their state.

For the third and fourth phases of this research, training materials, outlines, and descriptions from 25 law enforcement training programs were analyzed to identify common themes as well as unique and important topics. Materials were received from eight states (Alabama, Arizona, California, Florida, Michigan, New York, Texas, and West Virginia), the FBI and the National Organization of Black Law Enforcement (NOBLE). In addition, training programs from 15 other programs, described in a report from the Educational Development Center, were utilized in data analysis (Boston Police Department; Essex County, NJ; Education Development Center, MA; Maryland State Police; Connecticut State Police; Massachusetts Criminal Justice Training Council; Broward County Sheriff, FL; Bethel Park, PA; Anti-Defamation League/Dept. of Law and Public Safety, NJ; U.S. Dept. of Justice; International Association of Chiefs of Police; Federal Law Enforcement Training Center; Human Rights Resource Center, San Rafael, CA; and, Gays and Lesbians Opposing Violence) (Education Development Center, 1993).

FINDINGS

The data collection process revealed a wide range of willingness on the part of individuals and institutions to share training materials and perceptions regarding those materials, and the topic areas addressed. Personal communication with law enforcement representatives in almost every state produced a wide range of reactions including comments such as "[information on LGBT is] not in the curriculum. [We] don't address that in [name of state]. Maybe you do in New York" or "it's not a problem [though] I've heard some rumblings" and proactive statements such as "the sooner we get a handle on hate crimes [in this state], the sooner we can address global hate crimes" (Personal communications, October, 1996).

The findings are reported in two sections: reporting and training. The section on reporting includes data on laws and rules governing the reporting of hate crimes, including the forms used. The training section includes data from interviews with training officers and training materials.

Reporting Hate Crimes

The number of law enforcement agencies in each state ranges from four in Hawaii to 1793 in Pennsylvania. Of the 44 states who participated in the survey, the majority (61%) have 300 or fewer law enforcement agencies. Forty states (91%) had statewide Uniform Crime Report programs, generally located within the State Police Department (n = 22, 50%), however, several were located in other government agencies (n = 14, 32%), or separate UCR program (n = 3, 7%).

Twenty-three informants (52%) reported that local law enforcement agencies are mandated to report hate crimes to the state UCR program. The percentage of law enforcement agencies in each state that report hate crimes to either the state UCR program or directly to the FBI ranged from none (Hawaii) to 100% (California, Delaware, Illinois, Kansas, Louisiana, Maryland, Maine, Michigan, Minnesota, Montana, New Jersey, Nevada, Oklahoma, Oregon, Pennsylvania, Rhode Island, South Carolina, and Virginia). In all but three of the 23 states (Arizona, Iowa, and Utah) with mandatory reporting requirements, over 90% of law enforcement agencies comply and report hate crimes (Table 1). Conversely, of the 21 states without mandatory reporting requirements, few law enforcement agencies report hate crimes (the exceptions are Connecticut, Montana, North Dakota, Nevada, Oklahoma, South Carolina, Washington, and Wyoming). Twenty-four states (54%) request zero reporting from agencies.

The majority of states participating in this survey (n = 29, 66%) use an incident reporting form that is either the same as the FBI form (n = 16, 36%) or very similar (n = 13, 30%). The form used by these 29 states plus

TABLE 1. Mandatory Reporting Laws and Reporting Rates

Percentage of Law Enforcement Agencies that Report Hate Crimes to the state UCR office	State has a Mandatory Reporting Law	State does not have a Mandatory Reporting Law
100%	California, Delaware, Illinois, Kansas, Kentucky, Louisiana, Maryland, Maine, Michigan, Minnesota, New Jersey, Oregon, Pennsylvania, Rhode Island, Virginia	Montana, Nevada, Oklahoma, South Carolina
90-99%	Alabama, Idaho, Wisconsin	Connecticut, Washington
89-25%	Arizona, Iowa, Utah	North Dakota, Wyoming
0-24%		Alaska, Colorado, Georgia, Hawaii, Massachusetts, North Carolina, Nebraska, New Hampshire, New York, South Dakota, Vermont, West Virginia
unknown	Arkansas, Florida, Texas	

an additional 11 states allows hate crimes to be reported by motivation (i.e., ethnic, sexual orientation, religion). Florida has a very detailed hate crime reporting form which includes–in check-off box style–types of indicators (such as words, gestures, holiday, etc.), activities (such as destroy landscape, burn cross, blood, etc.), symbols (such as swastika, ritualistic, etc.), as well as detailed demographic information on the victim(s) and perpetrator(s).

Training on Hate Crimes

According to training officers in the 38 states that participated in the survey, law enforcement officers in thirty-two states (84%) had received some training on hate crimes, usually, at least in part, from the FBI or based on FBI materials.[3] In eleven states (29%), training on hate crimes was accomplished through inservices and during training for recruits, but more frequently (23 states, 61%), training on hate crimes was voluntary, inconsistent or absent.

In the 32 states in which officers received some training on hate crimes, training included information on UCR reporting, 18 states (56%) included information on cultural diversity, and in nine states (28%) sexual orientation was specifically addressed. In five states (16%), advocates from the lesbian, gay, and bisexual community conducted part of the hate crimes training (California, Massachusetts, Rhode Island, Texas, and Utah).

Training materials. The training materials or outlines received from 8 states, the FBI, NOBLE, and descriptions of 15 other programs supported a variety of training modalities including inservices, teleconferences, seminars, workshops, and workshop series. The time devoted to hate crimes training and related issues ranged from 1.5 to 32 hours. The materials received from the Educational Development Center (EDC) summarizing 15 law enforcement training programs generally provided inadequate information to determine if a program reflected the animus or discriminatory model. However, at least four of the 15 programs described by EDC discussed prejudice, and therefore, were probably based on the animus model. The materials received from other sources clearly reflected the animus model (California, FBI, NOBLE, and Texas).

More than half of the 25 training programs included sections on identifying and investigating hate crimes (n = 21, 84%), criminal and civil statutes (n = 18, 72%), and reporting (n = 16, 64%). In most of the training materials, identifying hate crimes is based on the officer identifying the perpetrator's bias against the victim, thus reflecting the animus model. Community issues (such as impact on the community, inclusion of the community to combat hate crimes, and importance of a community response) were also frequently addressed in law enforcement training (n = 17, 68%). Other topics addressed in law enforcement training included victim impact (n = 12, 48%), prejudice and discrimination (n = 9, 36%), and cultural diversity and sensitivity (n = 7, 28%).

Over half of the programs (n = 15, 60%) included some mention of sexual orientation in the training. Several programs had extensive information concerning hate crimes motivated by sexual orientation, including videotapes and community resources (for example, NOBLE). Others seemed only to note that sexual orientation was included in the federal UCR legislation. Only three programs specifically indicated that they use community advocates from various target groups in the training (California, Sacramento, and the International Association of Chiefs of Police), and only one indicated that they used advocates from the lesbian, gay, and bisexual community (California).

Model training programs. Eight respondents indicated that they believed they had at least one model program in their state (Arizona, California, Maine, Massachusetts, Michigan, New Jersey, Pennsylvania, and Utah). A model program could be described as one conducted within the paradigm of "working toward developing a culture of training that explores beliefs, values and customs that form the basis for . . . shared perceptions of social reality" (Herek, 1990, p. 319). Operating within this paradigm would allow law enforcement officers and trainers to "address the standard of denial and stigmatization that may be inherent to the culture of some police departments" (Personal communication, [name of law enforcement trainer], November, 1990). Model programs trained officers to pro-active, to understand the nature of prejudice, to understand the impact of hate crimes on the victim and community, and to work with the community to prevent, investigate and resolve hate crimes. The training programs submitted for review revealed several themes indicative of model training programs:

- cooperative educational agreements with leaders of gay and lesbian communities.
- emphasis on the significance of animus in perpetrators and law enforcement officers
- implementation of competency-based law enforcement training standards to identify crimes motivated by sexual orientation bias, and response to both individuals and the target community.

DISCUSSION AND RECOMMENDATIONS

The enactment of hate crimes legislation raised awareness of the severity of crimes motivated by animus toward individuals and communities, and the secondary impact of hate crimes on the surrounding society. States which mandate local law enforcement agencies to report hate crimes generally have high compliance rates; most states without mandatory reporting requirements have few law enforcement agencies that report these crimes. Therefore, it seems important that all states adopt mandatory reporting laws so that we can move one step closer to understanding the extent of this problem. Of course, mandatory reporting will not suffice if law enforcement officers do not understand hate crimes motivated by sexual orientation and thoroughly investigate them. The publication of FBI statistical information raised awareness in gay and lesbian communities that a disparity existed between the hate crimes data collected by law enforcement agencies and data collected by advocates positioned in the communities.

Although more than half of the training programs included sections on identifying and investigating, criminal and civil statutes, reporting, and community issues, fewer than half addressed victim impact, prejudice and discrimination, or cultural diversity and sensitivity. Based on the theoretical implications of understanding the animus of the crime, it seems essential that this content be included in law enforcement training on hate crimes. Effective law enforcement response should lead to a reduction in hate crimes, reduced victim trauma, and better relationships between law enforcement and the gay community (Education Development Center, 1993).

Even though most states and the FBI have aligned themselves theoretically with the animus model, training materials often reflect the discriminatory selection model and suggest that law enforcement communities do not understand that they are actually enforcing laws against criminal conduct that is grounded in the animus of the perpetrator (Lawrence, 1994). The alternative–grounding training materials in the animus model–would allow for a comprehensive review of the unique attributes of hate motivated crimes. Based in the animus model, training materials would increase attention to the impact of crime motivated by sexual orientation bias on the lives of gay and lesbian individuals (Lawrence, 1994).

Grounding law enforcement training in the animus model could have a significant impact on not only the training providers and recipients, but also on the community at large. Participating in an animus-focused educational experience with representatives of the gay and lesbian community has the potential to reduce negative perceptions of lesbian, gay, bisexual, and transgendered persons and facilitate the positive actions by law enforcement officers as they provide general and specialized interventions for gay and lesbian victims (Garnets, Herek, & Levy, 1990).

Beyond identifying and responding to the perpetrator's choice of victim, training materials must address the significance of the perpetrator's animus (a demonstration of prejudice) toward the target group, the gay and lesbian community. Training should include materials that teach law enforcement officers to discern between what happened and why it happened, within the context of their own biases. Law enforcement professionals must be aware of their own heterosexist biases and assumptions and should be familiar with current and accurate information about LGBT identity, differing responses to victimization (Harry, 1990), and community mental health concerns (Garnets, 1990). Law enforcement trainers and officers should make an effort to learn first hand from gay and lesbian individuals who have been victimized, and from advocates and service providers in the community.

NOTES

1. An example of discriminatory selection would be an offender who robs white victims because the offender believes white victims have more money (Lawrence, 1994).

2. In the racial animus model, an offender would select a victim because of hatred or animosity towards persons of a particular race or ethnicity (Lawrence, 1994).

3. This training did not include all officers in the state. Usually trainers or state UCR personnel were trained, and they then trained others in the state, upon request.

REFERENCES

Berk, R. (1990). Thinking about hate motivated crimes. *Journal of Interpersonal Violence, 5*(3), 334-349.

Berrill, K., & Herek, G. (1990). Introduction. *Journal of Interpersonal Violence, 5*(3), x-273.

Berrill, K., & Herek, G. (1992). Primary and secondary victimization in anti-gay hate crimes: Official response and public policy. In G. Herek & K. Berrill (Eds.), *Hate crimes: Confronting violence against lesbians and gay men* (pp. 289-305). Newbury Park, CA: Sage Publications, Inc.

Czajkoski, E. (1992). Criminalizing hate: An empirical assessment. *Federal Probation, 56*(3), 36-40.

Education Development Center. (1993). A Model Protocol and Training Curriculum to Improve the Treatment of Victims of Bias Crimes. Unpublished report. (Available from author, 55 Chapel Street, Newton, MA 02160).

Ehrlich, H. (1990). The ecology of anti-gay violence. *Journal of Interpersonal Violence, 5*(3), 359-365.

Freeman, S., & Kaminer, D. (1994). *Hate crimes laws: A comprehensive guide.* New York, NY: Anti-Defamation League.

Garnets, L., Herek, G., & Levy, B. (1990). Violence and victimization of lesbians and gay men. *Journal of Interpersonal Violence, 5*(3), 366-383.

Harry, J. (1990). Conceptualizing antigay violence. *Journal of Interpersonal Violence, 5*(3), 350-358.

Hate Crime Statistic Act. (1990). Public Law 101-275, § 104 Stat. 140 (1991).

Herek, G. (1992). The community response to violence in San Francisco: An interview with Wenny Kusuma, Lester Olmstead-Rose, and Jill Tregor. In G.

Herek & K. Berrill (Eds.), *Hate crimes: Confronting violence against lesbians and gay men* (pp. 241-258). Newbury Park, CA: Sage Publications.

Herek, G. (1990). The context of antigay violence: Notes on cultural and psychological heterosexism. *Journal of Interpersonal Violence, 5*(3), 316-333.

Herek, G. (1989). Hate crimes against lesbians and gay men. *American Psychologist, 44*(6), 948-955.

Herek, G., & Berrill, K. (1990). Documenting the victimization of lesbians and gay men: Methodological issues. *Journal of Interpersonal Violence, 5*(3), 301-315.

Herek, G., & Berrill, K. (1992). *Hate crimes: Confronting violence against lesbians and gay men.* Newbury Park, CA: Sage Publications.

Jenness, V. (1995). Social movement growth, domain expansion, and framing processes: The gay/lesbian movement and violence against gays and lesbians as a social problem. *Social Problems, 42*(1), 145-170.

Justice Research and Statistics Association (1996). *Directory of State Representatives.* Washington, DC.

Kibelstis, T. (1995). Preventing violence against gay men and lesbians: Should enhanced penalties at sentencing extend to bias crimes based on victims' sexual orientation? *Notre Dame Journal of Law, Ethics & Public Policy, 9*, 309-343.

Lawrence, F. (1994). The punishment of hate: Toward a normative theory of bias-motivated crimes. *Michigan Law Review, 93*, 320-381.

Mason, G. (1993). Violence prevention today: Violence against lesbians and gay men. *Violence Prevention Today Series, 2*, Australian Institute of Criminology.

National Gay and Lesbian Task Force (1996). *Lesbian, gay, and bisexual civil rights laws in the U.S.* Washington, DC: National Gay and Lesbian Task Force Policy Institute.

National Organization of Black Law Enforcement Executives (Producers), & Johnson, C. (Director). (1991). *Hate crime: A police perspective* [film]. (Available from Horizons in Video, 108 Elden Street, Suite 10, Herndon, VA 22070).

Saraceno, A. (1993). *Hate crimes against the lesbian, gay, and bisexual populations at a large midwestern university.* Unpublished manuscript, Illinois State University.

Shuman-Moore, E., Watts, D., & Giffels, M. (1995). Bias violence: Advocating for victims (part III). *Clearinghouse Review, 28*, 1228-47.

U.S. Department of Justice. (1994). *Hate crime statistics 1994.* Washington, DC: U.S. Government Printing Office.

U.S. Department of Justice. (1993). *Hate crime data collection guidelines.* Washington, DC: U.S. Government Printing Office.

U.S. Department of Justice. (date unknown a). *Training guide for hate crime data collection.* Washington, DC: U.S. Government Printing Office.

U.S. Department of Justice. (date unknown b). *Hate crime data collection guidelines.* Washington, DC: U.S. Government Printing Office.

Werthheimer, D. (1992). Treatment and service interventions for lesbian and gay male crime victims. In G. Herek & K. Berrill (Eds.), *Hate crimes: Confronting violence against lesbians and gay men* (pp. 227-240). Newbury Park, CA: Sage Publications.

Violence
and Lesbian and Gay Youth

Nora S. Gustavsson

Ann E. MacEachron

SUMMARY. Violence has become an increasingly common event in the lives of many adolescents. Lesbian and gay youth are subject to physical as well as non-physical forms of violence. This article explores multiple forms of violence and suggests strategies for addressing violence. *[Article copies available for a fee from The Haworth Document Delivery Service: 1-800-342-9678. E-mail address: getinfo@ haworthpressinc.com]*

Young people are often exposed to violence, either as victims or as observers, because violence is an intimate part of the environment. Adolescents may be exposed to or be a victim of domestic violence, violence in their communities, violence on television and through other mass media, and in the schools. Lesbian, gay, and bisexual young people face an increased risk of violence as a result of their sexual minority status.

The narrow definition of violence as physical force, or threat of physical force, to control and abuse misses many of the more subtle forms of violence. Being denied opportunities to fully participate in society or suffering nonphysical acts of humiliation can diminish self-esteem, under-

Nora S. Gustavsson, PhD, is Associate Professor, and Ann E. MacEachron, PhD, is Professor, both at the School of Social Work, Arizona State University, Tempe, AZ 85287-1802.

[Haworth co-indexing entry note]: "Violence and Lesbian and Gay Youth." Gustavsson, Nora S., and Ann E. MacEachron. Co-published simultaneously in *Journal of Gay & Lesbian Social Services* (The Haworth Press, Inc.) Vol. 8, No. 3, 1998, pp. 41-50; and: *Violence and Social Injustice Against Lesbian, Gay and Bisexual People* (ed: Lacey M. Sloan, and Nora S. Gustavsson) The Haworth Press, Inc., 1998, pp. 41-50. Single or multiple copies of this article are available for a fee from The Haworth Document Delivery Service [1-800-342-9678, 9:00 a.m. - 5:00 p.m. (EST). E-mail address: getinfo@ haworthpressinc.com].

mine self-confidence, and encourage a pervasive sense of insecurity and self-doubt.

Young people who are gay, lesbian, or bisexual are subject to multiple forms of violence, both physical and nonphysical. This article explores differing types of violence in the lives of young people, explores the harassment of gay and lesbian youth in school, and offers strategies for protecting lesbian, gay, and bisexual youth.

PHYSICAL VIOLENCE

To be young in America is to be at an elevated risk for violence. Young people are more likely to be victims of violent crime than are adults. Adolescents and young people are the most frequent victims of homicide, robbery, assault, and crimes of theft (U.S. Department of Justice, 1994a). Almost half of all victims of violent crime are between the ages of 12 and 25 with a third of the victims between the ages of 12 and 19 (U.S. Department of Justice, 1994b). The 12 through 19 year old age group comprises only about 14% of the population yet is victimized at a rate that far exceeds this number.

African American male adolescents are at the greatest risk. Homicide is the leading cause of death for this group of young people. In 1994, the majority (51%) of murder victims were black (U.S. Department of Justice, 1994a). Homicide is the second leading cause of death for all adolescents and young adults (Committee on Ways and Means, 1991).

The ready availability of firearms has had dire consequences for America's youth. A child dies every two hours from a gunshot wound (Children's Action Alliance, 1996). Many more youngsters suffer serious injury as a result of gunshot wounds. In Arizona, for example, for every adolescent fatally injured by a gun, another five are hospitalized. In the three year period between 1989 and 1992, the number of Arizona adolescent homicide victims doubled (Morrison Institute for Public Policy, 1994). More generally, ninety percent of the victims of gunshot wounds (from crime) are male, 60% are African American, and 25% are under the age of 25 (U.S. Department of Justice, 1996).

Violence is ubiquitous in some communities. There are neighborhoods in which one in four adolescents has witnessed a murder and almost 75% know someone who had been shot (Zinsmeister, 1990). Young children are also exposed to violence. A survey of 500 elementary school children reported that 40% had seen a shooting and another 34% had seen a stabbing (Children's Defense Fund, 1990).

The home continues to be a place of violence. In 1994, 16% of murder victims were killed by a member of their immediate family and another two thirds were killed by a friend or acquaintance (U.S. Department of Justice, 1994b). Child maltreatment reports exceed one million and 24% of the victims of maltreatment are between the ages of 12 and 18 (National Center on Child Abuse and Neglect, 1994).

Television and films are another source of environmental violence. While a causal relationship between observing violence and perpetrating violence is not established, there is evidence to suggest that viewing violence increases subsequent aggressive behaviors (Comstock & Strasburger, 1990). Young people spend many hours watching television and will over the course of their viewing years see approximately 180,000 murders, rapes, robberies, and assaults (Comstock & Strasburger, 1990).

Many adolescents live in a violent world. Lesbian and gay adolescents are not exempt from these manifestations of overt violence. Because of their sexual minority status, homophobia, and heterosexism, they may face an elevated risk for violence and experience forms of violence unique to their minority status. However, the invisibility of gays and lesbians makes it difficult to estimate the frequency of violence perpetrated against young people solely because of their sexuality (see Sloan in this volume). Each state can decide whether to have hate crime laws and which categories of people to include. Some battles are being fought at the state level as interest groups fight to include or exclude sexual minorities in hate crime reports.

VIOLENCE AND THE SCHOOL

The school setting could offer gay, lesbian, or bisexual adolescents a temporary haven where they could feel safe. Unfortunately, safety is elusive for sexual minority youth. Exact rates of incidence are unknown, but as many as half of lesbian and gay students may be physically harassed at school with more than 90% subject to verbal abuse (Gay, Lesbian, and Straight Teachers Network, 1996).

Lesbian and gay young people face nonphysical forms of violence on a daily basis. Living in a heterosexist and homophobic society results in messages such as gay and lesbian youth do not exist, or if they do exist, they are sick or sinful. These messages are communicated through channels such as the family, mass media, peers, religion, and schools. The messages provide an ideological base for discriminatory actions and supports the marginalization of sexual minority youth.

An arena which could be one of the few safe places for sexual minority youth may in fact be a major source of violence (O'Conor, 1994). Schools can tolerate, encourage, or perpetuate homophobia or take a position which supports and affirms gay and lesbian youth. But supporting sexual minority youth has been politicized. The Congress periodically debates the role of public schools in educating lesbian and gay youth. Amendments to forbid actions which could be seen as supporting deviant (gay and lesbian) lifestyles are offered periodically. The recent attention devoted to the Defense of Marriage Act (see Kopels this volume) attests to the politics of sexuality and the depth of homophobia.

It can be difficult for schools to support their gay and lesbian youth (Morrow, 1993). The homophobia of school boards, superintendents, administrative personnel, teachers, parents, and other students presents a formidable barrier to supporting lesbian and gay youth. The intolerance and fear which characterizes these many groups is translated into actions which diminish gay and lesbian youth. For example, schools may not permit books which refer to homosexuality, the homosexuality of famous historical figures can be omitted from the curriculum as can the contributions and history of the gay liberation movement. To add to this invisibility, school personnel in some states can be subject to dismissal for no other reason than their homosexual identity.

In addition to the invisibility which adds to the young person's sense of isolation, negative messages can be communicated. Males in particular use sexuality as a method of intimidation. Boys use words such as faggot and queer to insult each other. Coaches of boys sports may also use these terms as well as others. Coaches unhappy with performance may refer to the team members as girls or sissies. Coaches of girls teams are less likely to insult the girls by calling them names.

SEXUAL HARASSMENT

There are laws which forbid sexual harassment in specific areas such as the school and work place. However, sexual harassment is not equivalent to harassment based on sexuality. A more accurate term is gender harassment. Like all adolescents, gay, lesbian, and bisexual youth are subject to gender harassment as well as harassment based upon their sexuality.

Sexual harassment is defined as unwanted or unwelcomed sexual behavior. A federal law concerned with civil rights in the education arena, Title IX, prohibits sex discrimination. However, sexual harassment remains a serious problem in the schools. The Department of Education has established a division that deals with discrimination based on race and gender. The Office for Civil Rights is charged with enforcing Title IX.

The courts have also become involved in Title IX issues because litigation is one method for redress of civil rights complaints. An area that the courts and the Office for Civil Rights have addressed is the right of a student to enjoy educational opportunities. Sexual harassment interferes with this right and occurs when opportunities to engage in educational activities are conditional upon sexual favors or when a "hostile environment" interferes with the opportunity to enjoy educational benefits. In a litigious environment, operationalizing harassment and hostile environment is arduous.

A 1993 Harris Poll survey (n = 1600) reported that more than 80% of girls (ages 8 through 11) had experienced some form of sexual harassment (American Association of University Women). Large numbers of young people are subject to this pernicious form of violence. Resolving Title IX complaints of harassment by members of the opposite sex has been laborious. Victims of same sex harassment have received even less attention and protection.

Because sexuality is unprotected by federal regulation, it is legal to discriminate against persons because of their sexuality. Some municipalities have enacted legislation to extend limited protections to gay, lesbian, and bisexual adults. However, Title IX is of limited value to lesbian and gay students. Young people will not find redress if they claim they were harassed or suffered a hostile environment because they are gay or lesbian because sexuality is unprotected. Lesbian, gay, and bisexual students are better served by making a claim based on gender.

Boys may have an especially difficult time establishing sexual harassment claims as evidenced by court decisions. A case which received national attention occurred in Utah. The courts turned a deaf ear to the abuse of a boy by his fellow football team mates and coach. After a football game, the adolescent was taped to a towel rack when he left the shower. A female classmate was taken into the locker room against her will and forced to look at him. When the young man complained about the incident, he was dismissed from the football team. The coach, who reportedly knew of this team behavior, was not disciplined nor were any of the football players. School officials viewed the behavior as an adolescent hazing ritual and inappropriate for any disciplinary action. The federal courts agreed with the action (or lack thereof) of the school and ruled that the victim had not proven that he had been subject to concerted discrimination nor did he prove that the conduct of his abusers was sexual (Seamons v. Snow, 1994).

HOMOPHOBIA IN THE SCHOOLS

Some teachers and school districts try to create a safe environment for young people. Such actions can subject the school to attack. Safety for sexual minority youth may be viewed as support for deviance and feeds the fears of homophobes. For example, some high school teachers in a small Connecticut town place pink triangles on their classroom doors. This designated the classroom as a safety zone for lesbian, gay, and bisexual youth. The pink triangle program attracted attention in 1996 when the parents of one student complained and accused a teacher of recruiting for homosexuality and advancing the homosexual agenda (although the details of the homosexual agenda appear to be known to only a select group of non-homosexuals). The conflict created by the pink triangle program is so serious that court involvement is inevitable ("Open door policy," 1996).

A Utah school district made national news when the school board voted to ban extracurricular clubs. This action was a response to a group of lesbian and gay students who, with faculty advisors, had formed a support group. The state senate became involved in the conflict and passed a bill that prohibits teachers from condoning illegal conduct in schools ("Students protest club ban," 1996).

Many of the battles for sexual minority youth are being fought at the school board level. In New Hampshire, a policy which forbids teaching of homosexuality as a positive lifestyle has resulted in a federal lawsuit. The ban includes all grades and all schools within the district and in effect prohibits any activity or program which has the purpose or encourages or supports homosexuality as a positive lifestyle alternative (Loung, 1996).

This regulation challenges First Amendment rights to free speech and makes little pedagogical sense. Does this regulation require teachers to omit works by James Baldwin and Shakespeare? Can the Sistine Chapel and the works of gay and lesbian artists be discussed? Textbook battles are becoming increasingly common and important. Excluding material on lesbian and gay historical figures and events can add to a sense of isolation of sexual minority youth and supports homophobia (Kielwasser & Wolf, 1994).

One of the more bizarre examples of homophobia at the school level comes from Massachusetts. The parents of a 14 year old girl are suing the Brookline school district. The girl was traumatized by her social studies teacher when the teacher came out as a lesbian. The parents removed their daughter from the school and enrolled her in a Christian school. The parents are seeking more than $300,000 for tuition at the private school, medical bills, legal fees, and an additional $300,000 for emotional distress. The 14 year old girl did not feel the school was an emotionally safe environment since it sponsored a homosexuality awareness month with lesbian and gay affirming activities. She did not feel her traditional views were acceptable (Smith, 1996).

RESPONDING TO THE VIOLENCE

Messages which negate the uniqueness and minimize the value of gay and lesbian youth are a form of violence (Singer, 1996). The response to the diffuse and pervasive violence of homophobia and heterosexism can be to internalize the anger. Learned helplessness and a sense of powerlessness can also compromise emotional well-being (Seligman, 1975). Mental health professionals are familiar with these types of responses to societal violence. Suicide, self-destructive behaviors, and drug abuse are common examples (Hershberger & D'Augelli, 1995). Delinquency and other criminal behavior represents a misguided attempt to respond to the violence with counterviolence (Gil, 1996). It is often difficult for the victims of violence to be able to identify the source of the violence.

Americans appear comfortable with misdirected responses to societal violence and are willing to provide limited remedial services. Lesbian, gay, and bisexual youth can receive professional mental health services for depression and substance abuse. Social service agencies treat these issues as individual, personal problems with therapies designed to help the client cope. This inadvertently maintains the status quo, as the victims of societal violence are isolated and blamed for their own problems (Barber, 1995).

While individual lesbian, gay and bisexual youth may profit from therapy designed to help them strengthen their coping skills and increase their support network, other interventions may also be helpful. Creating and maintaining affirming and safe environments can prevent the development of pathological responses to societal violence. Exemplars of such environments exist across the country. The Los Angeles school system has a program (Project 10) for gay, lesbian and bisexual youth and curriculum materials for all schools. San Francisco has a similar program called Project 21. Massachusetts established a commission on gay and lesbian youth and now has policies which protect lesbian and gay students from harassment and discrimination and encourages the establishment of school-based support groups for gay and lesbian students. The commission also recognized the dangers of invisibility and encourages schools to include in their libraries and curriculum materials which acknowledge the contributions as well as the works of gays and lesbians (Governor's Commission on Gay and Lesbian Youth, 1993). New York City has a high school for lesbian, gay and bisexual youth.

All school districts need to be encouraged to protect vulnerable sexual minority youth (Zimmerman, 1996). This requires involvement at the local level. The political climate in Washington is not receptive to many of the issues of concern to lesbians and gays. Protecting young gays and lesbians will require concerned adults to attend school board hearings, vote carefully for school board members, and lobby at the state level for First Amendment rights.

Marginalization efforts do not appear to be attenuating. Legislation is being proposed in Arizona that would ban gay groups from public schools and university campuses. Specifically, it would forbid any group that "encourages criminal or delinquent behavior or involves human sexuality" from forming and requires schools to keep such organizations from meeting or having faculty sponsors (Mayes, 1996). Since sodomy is a felony in the state, the groups sponsoring this legislation can try to garner support for their position by saying they are protecting young people from criminals and criminal acts. In reality, youth need to be protected from the disaffirming, demoralizing and discriminatory actions of homophobic adults.

Organizations are confronting homophobia. In addition to national lesbian and gay rights groups (such as the Gay and Lesbian Alliance Against Defamation and the Gay and Lesbian Caucus of the National Education Association), Parents, Friends and Families of Lesbians and Gays (PFLAG) advocates for policies to end discrimination. The Gay, Lesbian, and Straight Teachers Network was founded in 1990 and is actively involved in challenging homophobia. Local gay community service centers can also play a role in making the schools safe by offering training and workshops on the needs and problems of lesbian and gay youth and monitoring school policies. They may also support sexual minority youth by offering recreational programs and mentoring.

A two-tiered approach includes programs to support individual lesbian, gay, and bisexual youth. On one level, counseling services (both individual and group) can be offered that address the unique needs of this population and which are provided in an affirming and supportive environment. On a second level, political action at the local level is necessary in order to confront homophobia in its ubiquitous forms, especially in the schools, and alter the environment to make it healthy for all youth.

REFERENCES

American Association of University Women. (1993). *Hostile hallways: The AAUW survey on sexual harassment in America's schools.* Washington, DC: Author.

Barber, J. G. (1995). Politically progressive casework. *Families in Society, 76*(1), 30-37.

Children's Action Alliance. (1996). *Changing the odds for Arizona's youth.* Phoenix, AZ: Author.

Children's Defense Fund. (1990). *S.O.S. America: A children's defense budget.* Washington, DC: Author.

Committee on Ways and Means. (1991). *1991 green book: Background material and data on programs within the jurisdiction of the Committee on Ways and Means* (Committee Print 102-109). Washington, DC: U.S. Government Printing Office.

Comstock, G., & Strasburger, V.C. (1990). Deceptive appearances: Television violence and aggressive behavior. *Journal of Adolescent Health Care, 11*(1), 31-44.

Gay, Lesbian, and Straight Teachers Network. (September, 1996). *Back to school campaign.* New York: Author.

Gil, D. G. (1996). Preventing violence in a structurally violent society: Mission impossible. *American Journal of Orthopsychiatry, 66*(1), 77-84.

Governor's Commission on Gay and Lesbian Youth. (1993). *Making schools safe for gay and lesbian youth: Breaking the silence in schools and in families.* Boston, MA: Author.

Hershberger, S. L., & D'Augelli, A.R. (1995). The impact of victimization on the mental health and suicidality of lesbian, gay, and bisexual youths. *Developmental Psychology, 31*(1), 65-74.

Kielwasser, A.P., & Wolf, M.A. (1994). Silence, difference, and annihilation: Understanding the impact of mediated heterosexism on high school students. *The High School Journal, 77,* 58-78.

Loung, S. (1996, February 16). School policy on gays prompts suit. *Boston Globe,* p. 25.

Mayes, K. (1996, December 24). Lawmakers targeting gay groups. *Arizona Republic,* pp. 1,7.

Morrison Institute for Public Policy. (1994). *Arizona's child and adolescent injury data book.* Tempe, AZ: Author.

Morrow, D. F. (1993). Social work with gay and lesbian adolescents. *Social Work, 38*(6), 655-660.

National Center on Child Abuse and Neglect. (1994). *Child maltreatment 1994: Reports from the states to the National Center on Child Abuse and Neglect.* Washington, DC: U.S. Department of Health and Human Services.

O'Conor, A. (1994). Who gets called queer in school? Lesbian, gay and bisexual teenagers, homophobia and high school. *The High School Journal, 77,* 7-12.

Open door policy. (1996, May 16). *Echo,* p. 15.

Seamons v. Snow, 864 F. Supp. 1111 (D. Utah, 1994).

Seligman, M.E.P. (1975). *Helplessness: On depression, development and death.* San Francisco, CA: Freeman.

Singer, C. (1996, August). Recognizing gay and lesbian youth: What can we do to help them grow up well adjusted? *Orange County and Long Beach Blade*, pp. 42-43.

Smith, P. (1996, March 15). Brookline suit looks silly. *Boston Globe*, p. 25.

Students protest club ban aimed at gay support groups. (1996, February 26). *Boston Globe*, p. 3.

U.S. Department of Justice. (1994a). *Criminal victimization 1994.* Washington, DC: Author.

U.S. Department of Justice. (1994b). *Murder in families, special report.* Washington, DC: Author.

U.S. Department of Justice. (1996). *Firearm injury from crime.* Washington, DC: Author.

Zimmerman, V. (1996, August). Making schools rainbow friendly. *Orange County and Long Beach Blade*, pp. 44-45.

Zinsmeister, K. (1990). Growing up scared. *The Atlantic Monthly, 265*(6), 49-66.

Prevalence of Suicide Attempts and Suicidal Ideation Among Lesbian and Gay Youth

Christine Flynn Saulnier

SUMMARY. Researchers argue that a disproportionate number of lesbian and gay adolescents attempt suicide. The problem demands careful attention from social work. Most, perhaps all, social workers serve lesbian and gay clients. Some are aware of it. Yet all too often social workers assume that the sexual orientation of the adolescents with whom they work does not vary. When that assumption is made, social workers may be missing a key opportunity to understand and intervene with and on behalf of gay and lesbian teens. This paper begins by defining several pertinent terms. Next, it examines findings concerning prevalence and risk factors for suicidality in lesbian and gay youth, and provides information on recognizing lesbian and gay adolescents. The paper ends with an overview of areas in which social workers need to intervene. *[Article copies available for a fee from The Haworth Document Delivery Service: 1-800-342-9678. E-mail address: getinfo@haworthpressinc.com]*

Several authors have examined suicide rates and determined that they are disproportionately high among lesbian and gay youth (Bell & Weinberg, 1978; Erwin, 1993; Gibson, 1989; Jay & Young, 1979).[1] In their

Christine Flynn Saulnier, PhD, is Assistant Professor, Boston University, School of Social Work, States Way, Boston, MA 02214.

[Haworth co-indexing entry note]: "Prevalence of Suicide Attempts and Suicidal Ideation Among Lesbian and Gay Youth." Saulnier, Christine Flynn. Co-published simultaneously in *Journal of Gay & Lesbian Social Services* (The Haworth Press, Inc.) Vol. 8, No. 3, 1998, pp. 51-68; and: *Violence and Social Injustice Against Lesbian, Gay and Bisexual People* (ed: Lacey M. Sloan, and Nora S. Gustavsson) The Haworth Press, Inc., 1998, pp. 51-68. Single or multiple copies of this article are available for a fee from The Haworth Document Delivery Service [1-800-342-9678, 9:00 a.m. - 5:00 p.m. (EST). E-mail address: getinfo@haworthpressinc.com].

study of 5,000 lesbians and gay men, Jay and Young (1979) found that 40 percent of the men and 39 percent of the lesbians had seriously considered or actually attempted suicide. Bell and Weinberg's survey of approximately 1,000 lesbians and gay men also found high percentages of people who had attempted or seriously contemplated suicide: 35 percent of gay men and 38 percent of lesbians seriously contemplated suicide, with 25 percent of the women and 20 percent of the men actually making attempts. Gibson argued that suicide is the leading cause of death among this population, with gay males being more than six times as likely to attempt suicide as heterosexual males (Gibson, 1989). Proctor and Groze (1994) studied 221 lesbian and gay youths who attended youth groups. They indicated that two thirds of their sample had attempted suicide.

These figures have been called into question of late (Muerher, 1995). The research methods used in the studies and the difficulty of operationalizing sexual orientation were cited as reasons for doubting the generalizability and validity of these figures. The retrospective nature of the reports, the involvement of many of the youths in social service systems, and the recruitment of study participants from bars may help to explain the large number of reported attempts. It is reasonable to argue that we are uncertain about the actual rates of suicide among lesbian and gay youth. It is not reasonable, however, to wait until we have accurate figures on incidence to develop prevention and intervention strategies, although our strategies must be adapted as new evidence appears. Muerher (1995) argued that the best way to help young people in distress is through early identification and treatment of the problems, whether the problem is suicidality or other problems often associated with suicidality: drug and alcohol abuse and mental illness.

The next section discusses risk factors for suicide, but the suggested intervention strategies that follow are meant to address a broad range of problems faced by lesbian and gay adolescents. Social workers are reminded that even when a disproportionate rate of suicidality was found among lesbian and gay adolescents, most studies found that a majority of lesbian and gay youths are not suicidal; we should take care to avoid over-pathologizing them.

RISK FACTORS

As with heterosexuals, gays and lesbians are more at risk for suicide in their youth. Most attempts occur prior to age 21. One third occur before age 17 (Gibson, 1989). Schneider, Farberow, and Kruks (1989) found that among boys, the mean age at first attempt was 16.3 years. Attempts are often linked with sexual milestones (Savin-Williams, 1994). Level of risk also seems to be related to the age at which a girl or boy comes out, with younger age being a higher risk (Roesler & Deisher, 1972, as cited in Schneider, Farberow, & Kruks, 1989). This may be due, in part, to emotional immaturity and related inability to respond to ostracism. It also appears to be associated with insufficient access to positive information concerning lesbian and gay people (Gibson, 1989).

Schneider, Farberow, and Kruks (1989) indicated that most suicide attempters were still closeted at the time of their first attempt, and that those who were coming out had experienced rejection. Unfortunately, many helping professionals still tend patronizingly to dismiss lesbian and gay feelings as a passing phase, despite evidence that sexual orientation is formed by adolescence (Gibson, 1989).

Race and gender differences have been found: Whites seem more likely than Blacks, women more likely than men, and lesbians and gays more likely than heterosexuals to attempt or seriously contemplate suicide. The lowest risk group appears to be heterosexual, black men; the highest, white lesbians. Bell and Weinberg (1978) noted that although blacks were less likely than whites to attempt suicide, those blacks who were suicidal were more likely to make attempts at an early age.

Stressful life events are often similar for suicidal gay and heterosexual youth, but the former have an additional set of stressors specific to their sexual orientation, including ridicule, and both intended and unintended disclosure of their orientation (Savin-Williams, 1994). The role of alcohol is important to consider in youth suicide more generally, and no less so with lesbian and gay youth (Rittner, Smyth, & Wodarski, 1995). Paternal alcohol problems are more likely to be found among suicidal gay youths (Garfinkle and colleagues, as cited in Schneider, Farberow, & Kruks, 1989). The combination of having an alcoholic father and a history of family violence seems particularly dangerous. In Schneider and colleagues' study of 108 members of a gay and lesbian college and community organizations, all of the gay men who reported histories of both alcoholic fathers and physical abuse within the family were suicidal (Schneider, Farberow, & Kruks, 1989).

Parental problems with alcohol are not the only concern. Savin-Williams (1994, p. 265) speculated that lesbian and gay youth overuse alcohol in an attempt to shelter themselves from the pain of social rejection based on their sexual orientation: "to fog an increasing awareness that they are not heterosexual, to defend against the painful realization that being lesbian or gay means a difficult life lies ahead, and to take refuge against parents and society for rejecting them." Bars sometimes function as the community entry point for young lesbians and gays (Savin-Williams, 1994) and it is not unusual for communities, particularly in smaller cities, to be lacking in socializing opportunities other than bars. This may encourage youth to focus on activities that have a heavy emphasis on alcohol, a less-than-desirable entry into lesbian and gay culture (Robinson, 1991). Caution must be used in interpreting the role of bars for adolescents. Bloomfield (1993) recently found that the long-suspected overuse of bars by adult lesbians is an inaccurate stereotype. We do not have data on lesbian and gay youth's use of bars.

Research indicates that there is no direct association between lesbian or gay orientation and psychopathology (Gonsiorek, 1991; Hooker, 1957; Proctor & Groze, 1994; Schneider, Farberow, & Kruks, 1989). The psychiatric symptoms that do appear tend to be explained in social or sociopolitical rather than psychological terms (Erwin, 1993; Gibson, 1993; Proctor & Groze, 1994; Remafedi, 1990). Gibson argued that heterosexism and homophobia make gay and lesbian youth more vulnerable to a number of psychosocial problems, including substance abuse and suicide: in his 1989 study of youth suicide for the Department of Health and Human Services, Gibson (1989, p. 3-126) cautioned: "it is a sobering fact to realize that we are the greatest risk factors in gay youth suicide."

Robinson (1991) reported that 70 percent of gay and lesbian youths identified their primary problem as isolation. Few opportunities exist for them to socialize. Gibson (1989) argued that meeting places for young lesbians are particularly scarce, that casual sexual contact is less likely between women than between men, and that these factors may lead lesbians to be even more isolated than young gay men. This may also help explain why lesbians tend to come out at a later age than gay males (Gibson, 1989). Given the difference in cultural expectations for girls, lesbians may have different suicide risks than gay male youth (Remafedi, Farrow, & Deisher, 1991), and suicidality in lesbians may stem, in part, from isolation and despair concerning contact with similar others (Gibson, 1989). Many adolescents report feelings of alienation, but for lesbian and gay youth, the problem seems to be more extensive. For example, Savin-Williams (1994) found that over 95% said they frequently felt separated and emotionally isolated from peers because of feeling different.

For adolescent members of other minority groups, it may be self-evident that positive role models are needed, from whom the youth can receive support, validation and examples of how to incorporate their stigmatized identity in a healthy way. For lesbian and gay youth, role models are not so readily available, both because they are unlikely to have been born into a family in which the adults are lesbian or gay, and because unrelated lesbians and gay men usually remain unavailable to them until adulthood. Often adults cannot risk sponsoring or participating in a youth event, for fear of being seen as "recruiting" gay and lesbian youth (Gibson, 1989). Adults often fall victim to what Martin (1982, p. 54) calls "one of the most destructive charges brought against [lesbians and gay men] that they are somehow a danger to children."

Researchers find that it is variables such as familial alcohol problems, childhood physical abuse, and anti-gay social attitudes, *not* lesbian or gay identity, per se, which are associated with suicidal ideation (Schneider, Farberow, & Kruks, 1989). Histories of abuse are as likely to be present among lesbian suicide attempters as among heterosexual attempters (Saulnier & Miller, forthcoming). As with other youths, the sexual abuse which may be found tends to have occurred in the home (Savin-Williams, 1994). Among runaways, gay and lesbian youth report a higher incidence of verbal and physical abuse in the home and they are more often "pushaways" or "throwaways" than runaways (Gibson, 1989).

Nor is school a safe haven. Nearly half of gay boys and a quarter of lesbian girls reported to The National Gay Task Force that they had experienced verbal or physical assault in school. Gibson calls junior and senior high schools "the brutal training grounds where traditional social roles are rigidly enforced" (1989, p. 3-117). It is no wonder that gays and lesbians sometimes choose truancy or dropping out in response to an unsafe learning environment. Harassment often is allowed, and in some cases even encouraged, by faculty or staff (Morrow, 1993; Savin-Williams, 1994).

SOCIAL WORK INTERVENTION
WITH LESBIAN AND GAY ADOLESCENTS

Recognizing the Lesbian or Gay Adolescent

The first step is individual acknowledgment of the existence of lesbian and gay adolescents. The second step is identification of those who may need help. It is not possible to determine by simple observation who is or is not heterosexual, bisexual, lesbian or gay. One cannot "spot" a gay or lesbian person accurately (Berger, Hank, Rauzi, & Simkins, 1987). Although stereotypes are common, the use of such inadequate criteria as dress, mannerisms, lifestyle, etc., will result in both false identification of some heterosexual youth as lesbian or gay and in false identification of some lesbian and gay youth as heterosexual. Most lesbian and gay adolescents do not exhibit gender-deviant behavior. What sometimes occurs is provocative or defiant behavior in situations perceived as heterosexist (Anderson, 1994). This is exemplified by the ACT-UP slogan, "We're here. We're queer. Get used to it," probably good advice for social workers and society as a whole.

Remafedi (1990) argued that to assess sexual orientation, one would need to assess fantasies, emotional or romantic attractions, and identification with heterosexual or with gay or lesbian people and communities, as well as sexual attractions. Most adolescents choose to pass as heterosexual while they are in high school (Savin-Williams, 1994). Given the rewards for appearing "normal," it is not surprising that most adolescents who are able to pass as heterosexual choose to do so (Martin, 1982). Nor can a social worker rely solely on knowledge of an adolescent's sexual activity to recognize a gay or lesbian youth. At least one study found that three quarters of adolescents who identified as gay or lesbian had histories of heterosexual intercourse (Boxer et al., 1989, cited by Anderson, 1994).[2] Remafedi pointed out the danger in requiring a "sexual litmus test" to resolve the question of sexual orientation, in light of the incidence of sexually transmitted diseases, particularly AIDS (Remafedi, 1990).

To recognize gay and lesbian youth, social workers need to give a clear message that it would be acceptable and safe to come out. Social workers need to ask about sexual orientation regularly, particularly once some rapport has been established. There is no reason to expect that an intelligent, rational adolescent will disclose such potentially dangerous information in untested waters. Indeed, clinicians may have legitimate concern about their emotional boundaries if they did.

Social workers are trained to detect and oppose discrimination. That training is useful here. For example, when asking adolescents whether they have experienced any harassment or unfair treatment because of their gender, ethnicity, etc., social workers should inquire about whether youths have been subjected to bias related to their sexual orientation.

Clinical Intervention

Individual Work

Suicide intervention efforts may best be directed at the time when sexual milestones are passed, that is, when youth are exploring their sexual identity, which may be as young as grade school (D'Augelli & Hershberger, 1993), and experiencing their first sexual contacts, typically during junior or senior high school, especially for women, during undergraduate years (Gibson, 1989; Remafedi, Farrow, & Deisher, 1991). A large part of the social worker's task may be to help them come out, recognizing, however, that coming out is not a panacea: "no myth is more dangerous to gay adolescents than the notion that 'coming out' will ensure them against feelings of self-destructiveness" (Gibson, 1989, p. 3-121, citing Rofes, 1983). It will not.

Questions about suicidal ideation must be asked of any adolescent in treatment, and for gay and lesbian youth it would be important to assess whether there are any problems associated with coming out or being out. Gibson (1989) recommended that during intake, or during the initial assessment of areas that affect the adolescent's life, for example, family, school, substance use, and depression, questions about sexuality should be asked directly as a matter of course. More general discussions of adolescent suicide clarify that silence is not the answer. Rather, ongoing attention to suicide assessment and specific probes for thoughts of self-harm are recommended (Ivanoff & Smyth, 1992; Rittner, Smyth & Wodarski, 1995).

It is important for clinicians to be informed and to actively counteract the perception that youth have of helping professionals as uncomfortable and homophobic (Sears, 1993, as cited in Reynolds & Koski, 1994). It is the social worker's duty to convince the adolescent that the worker is sensitive to the needs of lesbian and gay youth. Social workers need to be familiar enough with community resources that, if requested, they could make referrals to services or other practitioners with expertise in lesbian and gay issues (Gibson, 1989).

Because of heterosexism, lesbian and gay youth are confronted with multiple problems, only some of which are also experienced by heterosexual youth. They must develop a positive understanding of themselves within an environment that: (1) is often hostile to their self-definition; (2) frequently supplies a multitude of negative social images; and (3) responds disapprovingly to their inquiries about themselves. Often lesbian and gay youth must build a support system in spite of rejection by significant others; and they must create for themselves a positive sense of social belonging despite, at best, a lack of guidelines and, at worst, a clear message that there is no place where they belong (Gibson, 1989).

The problem is compounded for lesbian and gay youth from racial and ethnic minority groups. Morales (1990), reporting on the findings of the Human Rights Commission of San Francisco, recounted that institutionalized racism found in mainstream communities is reflected among lesbians and gays. At the same time that adolescents risk their sense of protection as ethnic persons, by coming out to their nuclear and often extended family, they might simultaneously encounter racism in the lesbian and gay community.

Remaining closeted is often a poor solution, however. Although confronting heterosexism can be dangerous and painful, the price of being closeted is also high, in terms of postponing emotional and identity development, compromising integrity, remaining vigilant against disclosure, and postponing membership in a relevant reference group (Gibson, 1989; Martin, 1982). Remaining closeted often means that membership in reference groups is based on a lie: the unchallenged assumption of heterosexuality (Martin, 1982). There is no clear solution that is appropriate for all or most adolescents.

Specific Interventions

Proctor and Groze (1994) found that lesbian and gay youths who had neither attempted nor considered suicide had personal and environmental characteristics that helped them cope with isolation and discrimination. These included high functioning family and support systems, and positive self-perception. They suggest that these may be productive targets of prevention and intervention.

Given the young age at which suicidal ideation can appear, it is necessary to assess and intervene early in the intervention process and early in the adolescent's life. This means asking at intake whether there are problems related to sexual orientation and it means intervening at both junior and senior high school levels. This is not to say that adolescents should be pressured to come out. They should not. They may have a very accurate perception that disclosure could result in explosive confrontations, in seriously damaged family relationships and even in loss of their home (Gibson, 1989; Remafedi, 1990). Morrow (1993) encouraged clinicians to fully explore with youths the possible repercussions (both positive and negative) of coming out to their families, particularly in light of adolescents' generally limited financial means. The youth's need for personal integrity and for honest, appropriate self-disclosure must be weighed against the possibility of becoming homeless before they are capable of providing for themselves, should they be rejected by their families and communities. Accurate assessment is key and should include careful attention to the benefits and liabilities of coming out to their families.

If an adolescent comes out to a social worker, Gibson advises clinicians to: (a) voice acceptance of the adolescent's self-identification, (b) acknowledge the difficulty involved in the decision to come out, (c) acknowledge the trust demonstrated by the disclosure, and (d) let the adolescent know the clinician still cares about them to counteract the usual rejection experienced after disclosure. If youths express confusion about their sexual orientation, that should be acknowledged as well, and they should be reassured that it is fine to be confused. They do not need to label themselves as lesbian, gay, bisexual or heterosexual, nor do they have to adopt a particular lifestyle or set of mannerisms. As usual, it is helpful to use their term for referring to themselves (gay, lesbian, bi, queer) and for referring to their significant other, if they have one (friend, partner, lover, girlfriend, boyfriend, et cetera).

Social workers must learn the terms that lesbian, gay, and bisexual (LGB) youth use, remembering that terms can vary by geographic location, ethnicity, race, and gender. It is important to ask questions that indicate an openness to variations in sexual orientation, for example, "Is your partner (lover/date) a boy or a girl?" Social workers can also be careful to use non-heterosexist language (Bieschke & Matthews, 1996), for example, partner or lover instead of boyfriend or girlfriend. Social workers should also monitor the tendency to speak as if all dating is heterosexual (Reynolds & Koski, 1994).

Group Work

Youth support groups for lesbians and gays can help reduce the isolation and loneliness lesbian and gay adolescents often report (Proctor & Groze, 1994). Facilitated groups can help identify and refer youths in need of additional services to other programs or agencies. Targeted groups are not always possible due to social and political climate or an inadequate number of participants. In these cases, group workers must avoid isolating a lesbian or gay youth in a group of heterosexuals. At the same time it would be unwise to ignore the enormous potential of groups to end social isolation.

As an alternative, it can be quite helpful to refer gay and lesbian youth to community social support groups. Although the social worker is more likely to find an accessible lesbian or gay community in a medium or large city, they are found in small cities as well. It would be useful to determine whether the adult community could function as a resource, providing recreation or support to adolescents who are out, as an adjunct to social work intervention (Robinson, 1991).

Specific Interventions

There are several ways to approach groups. Lesbian and gay adolescents can be included in groups with heterosexuals; groups can be designed specifically for lesbians and gays or they can be referred out to organizations that already have such groups. Morrow (1993) argued that more support groups are needed to supplement the limited number now available to lesbian and gay youth. She suggested developing groups for parents as well. Morrow maintained that social workers can play a key role in ensuring that such groups are developed in family service agencies, religious organizations, and schools.

Family Work

Families may need education and assistance in learning to adjust to raising a lesbian or gay child in a world that holds their offspring in disdain. Not only must parents let go of their heterosexual expectations (Uribe, 1994), but there may also be grief work for the parents to accomplish, both in terms of letting go of their perception of their daughter or son as heterosexual and their desire to become grandparents (Remafedi, 1990). Gibson (1989, p. 3-141) recommended that clinicians assure gay and lesbian youth that they will have families as adults, although their families are not likely to resemble the restrictive definition common today.[3] They are more likely to be composed of some biological/legal family members, life partner or lover, and friends and other close community members.

Parental education should include information about the futility of trying to alter sexual orientation as well as the potential harm that their own heterosexism could have (Gibson, 1989). Parents may also want to know about religious publications that address lesbian and gay issues (Malyon, 1981). Several references are included at the end of the article. Additionally, lesbian and gay youth should be helped to understand that a parent's initial inability to accept their orientation often changes with time and does not signify, necessarily, a lack of love or a rejection of the child (Gibson, 1989).

Social workers might also consider offering support and information groups to family members. Remafedi (1990) advised offering specific education and support for parents, as they are often ill equipped to respond to the news of a lesbian or gay offspring. He maintains that it is unusual for parents to be able to provide appropriate support and guidance for lesbian and gay children without assistance, and that most parents need information about non-heterosexual orientation.

Family service agency workers are probably well aware that poor family interaction is a risk for suicide and other mental health problems. Difficulty in accepting a youth's sexual orientation can contribute to negative interactions within a family and social workers need to be able to identify and intervene in these problems (Proctor & Groze, 1994).

Specific Interventions

Compared to the number of services available to lesbian and gay youth, which is insufficient, service availability for families is even more bleak (Proctor & Groze, 1994). An international advocacy organization that provides family services is P-FLAG (Parents and Friends of Lesbians and Gays). P-FLAG has developed a reading list for parents of lesbians and gays. Contact information and reading lists are provided in the resource list at the end of this article.

Schools and Social Support

School social workers can contribute significantly through advocacy, and support of non-discriminatory policies, and active promotion of inclusion of lesbian and gay youth in social activities (Gibson, 1989; Uribe, 1994). While it is undeniably dangerous for school personnel to be openly lesbian or gay and intervening in heterosexism can place people at risk, allowing attacks against lesbian and gay students to occur is even more dangerous. "Such attacks, if allowed to progress without protest, force the public school systems to concede to the wishes of those who foster negativism about homosexuality, thus contributing to the increased risk of suicide for some youths" (Proctor & Groze, 1994, p. 510). Those lesbian and gay teachers who cannot be out, along with heterosexual supporters, can still be encouraged to act as role models by actively confronting heterosexism (Reynolds & Koski, 1995).

Interventions in Other Non-Specialized Organizations

Proctor and Groze (1994) pointed out that lesbian and gay organizations that have support from social service agencies, various levels of government, churches and schools are better equipped to withstand criticism and conservative backlash. Social workers can play a key role in garnering some of that support.

While offering separate activities is a necessary first step, and probably an ongoing need, social workers should be wary of ghettoizing. Not only is separate rarely equal, but it may reinforce the cultural message that heterosexual youth need to be protected from lesbian and gay youth and that anything other than heterosexual orientation is beyond the pale. In Morgan Hill, CA, GLAS (Gay/Lesbian Advocacy and Support) (Berger & Purchin, 1995) was developed as a service of a larger agency. Funded by the United Way and sponsored by a multiservice community mental health center, GLAS was created by two openly gay staff: a social worker and a counselor. They provide individual counseling services and a weekly support meeting. The group is advertised in local high school newspapers. The multiservice center has a supportive administration who agreed to handle any community complaints. Berger and Purchin (1995) reported that after a year of operation there was only one such complaint.

Other things social workers can do from within organizations that serve a more general population are: (1) Make contact with service organizations that provide LGB specific services, (2) Formalize the connections between your agency and these services, to improve mutual referrals and to strengthen the credibility, support and resources available to the organizations; if none exist, (3) Develop a program in your agency, (4) Start with a support group, (5) Have LGB affirmative books, magazines, posters, community announcements and other symbols of support in offices and waiting areas (Reynolds & Koski, 1994; Vergara, 1984) (Anecdotal evidence suggests that these indications of support contribute greatly to a sense of belonging and support.), (6) Advertise the service, specifically mentioning lesbian and gay youth (Bieschke & Matthews, 1996), (7) Act as a liaison between LGB community as a whole and your organization, (8) Be knowledgeable about HIV and AIDS and prepared to counter myths about LBG people (Reynolds & Koski, 1995), (9) Document by age, gender and sexual orientation any services you provide and services that are needed but unfulfilled. (For confidentiality reasons, assign a case number, but do not include a name) (Reynolds & Koski, 1995), (10) Bring the met and unmet need to the attention of your agency's administrators. This may be easier for social workers than teachers, as we are bound by the NASW Code of Ethics to avoid discrimination and to actively seek to eliminate it,[4,5] (11) Provide public education via speaking engagements that address lesbian and gay issues (Proctor & Groze, 1994), (12) Help develop peer counseling and support telephone lines, and (13) Help sensitize staff at youth shelters, foster care and adoption services, residential and other programs to the needs of lesbian and gay youth and the special risks they face.

Culturally competent practice includes a focus on gay, lesbian and bisexual youths (Proctor & Groze, 1994). To facilitate cultural competence, social workers need to keep up-to-date on needs and occurrences in lesbian and gay communities. Many mid- to large-sized cities have community newspapers which help in this regard. Small, local bookstores that specialize in women's, progressive, and/or lesbian and gay selections often carry these community papers. Social workers can help develop non-discrimination policies in their agencies and in professional social work organizations and insist that they be enforced across all levels from national professional organizations to small, local agencies (Vergara, 1984). Lesbian and gay social workers can participate actively in lesbian and gay interest groups within NASW, CSWE and other social work professional organizations. Heterosexual social workers can contact the same groups for specific guidance on what is needed.

Societal Change

In addition to recognition at the levels of individual practitioner, schools, social service agencies, and national organizations, lesbian and gay youth need to be recognized on a societal level. Gibson (1989) argued that cultural discrimination, stigmatization, and denial of the presence of lesbian and gay youth are at the root of the problem of lesbian and gay youth suicide. Instead of using a victim-blaming approach which locates the problem of suicidality in the individual gay or lesbian adolescent, it would be more productive to acknowledge the ways in which social institutions, large and small, contribute to the problem (Erwin, 1993). Several approaches for ameliorating the problems are needed. Social workers should promote positive images of lesbians and gays and seek remedies for heterosexism (Erwin, 1993; Gibson, 1989). Incremental change which focuses on adding civil rights and protective legislation, and eliminating legal prohibitions against sexual activity, marriage or other ordinary social interactions among gays and lesbians may be necessary initial steps, but they are not sufficient (Vaid, 1995). More profound changes are needed. As with any oppressed group, it will be necessary for fundamental changes in society to take place, in which heterosexual orientation is no longer prescribed as the only acceptable option. Narrow parameters around family forms and modes of defining and accessing social services and economic resources need to change. That is, heterosexuality can no longer be the basis upon which society is organized.

A cautionary note is in order. It is not safe to assume that legislative progress for adults will have an equal effect on adolescents. For example, in Minnesota, legislation outlawing discrimination in housing and employment included language that prohibited teaching about homosexuality in public schools, and maintained specific discriminatory practices in voluntary organizations "that provide friends, counselors, or role models to youth," thus denying to youth the opportunity to work with gay or lesbian role models (Halvorsen, 1993, as cited in Kielwasser & Wolf, 1994, p. 62). Kielwasser and Wolf argued that the law condemns the symptoms while promoting the cause. Instead, we should include lesbian and gay adults as targets of our active recruitment of diverse, positive role models for youth (Gibson, 1989; Morrow, 1993).

Finally, on a societal level, it is vital that accurate information be distributed to any adults who work with adolescents, informing them of the presence and needs of gay and lesbian youth (Gibson, 1989). Diversity in sexual orientation should be included in discussions of normal development. Rather than promoting tolerance, social workers should encourage support, acceptance, and affirmation (Reynolds & Koski, 1994).

CONCLUSION

Lesbian and gay youth appear to be at disproportionately high risk for suicide. The primary contributing factor seems to be heterosexism. To intervene effectively, a social worker must be prepared to do more than provide case work, group work, or family interventions. First, the population must be acknowledged and recognized at individual, school or agency, and societal levels. Second, intervention efforts must include assistance in coming out safely and effectively combating heterosexism. Attempting to help the adolescent adapt to this social dysfunction is not recommended. Third, the social worker must engage in changing the circumstances which support heterosexism, that is, the social worker should actively engage in both policy and clinical interventions aimed at reducing heterosexism and making adolescents' social world one in which they *can* live as who they are.

RESOURCES

Readings for Parents

Many of these are on the recommended reading list of P-FLAG.

Aarons, L. (1995). *Prayers for Bobby: A mother's coming to terms with the suicide of her gay son.* San Francisco, CA: Harper.
Bernstein, R. (1995). *Straight parents/gay children: Keeping families together.* Emeryville, CA: Thunder's Mouth Press.
Coville, B. (Ed.). (1995). *Am I blue? Coming out from the silence.* New York: Harper Collins.
Dew, R. F. (1995). *The family heart: A memoir of when our son came out.* New York: Ballantine Books.

Due, L. (1995). *Joining the tribe: Growing up gay & lesbian in the '90s.* New York: Anchor Books.

Fricke, A. (1992). *Sudden strangers: The story of a gay son and his father.* New York: St. Martin's Press.

Grima, T. (1995). *Not the only one. Lesbian and gay fiction for teens.* Boston: Alyson.

Heron, A. (1995). *Two teenagers in twenty: Writings by gay and lesbian youth.* Boston: Alyson Publications.

Jennings, K. (1994). *Becoming visible: A reader in gay & lesbian history for high school & college students.* Boston: Alyson.

Marcus, E. (1993). *Is it a choice? Answers to 300 of the most frequently asked questions about gays and lesbians.* San Francisco, CA: Harper.

Massachusetts Governor's Commission on Gay and Lesbian Youth. (1995). *Gay and lesbian student rights resource guide.* Boston, MA: Author (State House, Rm. 111, Boston 02133).

Sherrill, J. (1994). *The gay, lesbian, and bisexual students' guide to colleges, universities, and graduate schools.* New York: New York University Press.

Woog, D. (1995). *School's out: The impact of gay and lesbian issues on America's schools.* Boston: Alyson.

Religious Publications

Boswell, J. (1980). *Christianity, social intolerance, and homosexuality.* Chicago: University of Chicago Press.

Cook, A. (1988). *And God loves each one: A resource for dialogue about the church and homosexuality.* Washington, DC: Task Force on Reconciliation, Dumbarton.

Matt, H. (1978). *The church and the homosexual.* New York: Pocket Books.

Pennington, S. (1978). *But Lord, they're gay.* Hawthorne, CA: Lambda Christian Fellowship.

Scanzoni, L., & Mollenkott, V. (1978). *Is the homosexual my neighbor? Another Christian view.* San Francisco: Harper.

Directories and National Organizations

You Are Not Alone: National Lesbian, Gay and Bisexual Youth Organization Directory, Spring 1993. Write: Directory, Hetrick-Martin Institute, 401 West Street, New York, NY 10014 ($5).

Federation of Parents and Friends of Lesbians and Gays (P-FLAG) Inc., PO Box 27605, Washington, DC 20038-7605–over 200 chapters in US and Canada.

Gay, Lesbian and Straight Teachers Network (GLSTN) (212) 727-0135; 122 West 26th Street, Suite 1100, New York, NY 10001; e-mail: glstn@glstn.org

National AIDS Information Clearinghouse (800) 458-5231.

National Gay and Lesbian Task Force, Washington, DC (202) 332-6483.

Internet Resources

1. INTERNATIONAL LESBIAN AND GAY YOUTH ASSOCIATION
   <url://gopher://uclink.berkeley.edu:1901/11/other/intern/iglyo>

2. PARENTS AND FRIENDS OF LESBIANS AND GAYS (P-FLAG)
   <url://gopher://uclink.berkeley.edu:1901/00/other/national-orgs/
   pflag/pflag>

3. NATIONAL GAY AND LESBIAN TASK FORCE
   <url://gopher://uclink.berkeley.edu:1901/11/other/national-orgs/ngltf>

4. GAY, LESBIAN, AND STRAIGHT TEACHERS NETWORK
   (GLSTN)
   http://www.glstn.org/freedom/

NOTES

1. Kielwasser and Wolf argued that "While suicide among lesbian and gay youth is not uncommon, the statistical profiles used to document a high rate of suicidality are problematic." Since it is virtually impossible to obtain a random sample of any stigmatized group, samples tend to be used on clinical populations, with all the obvious implications for bias. This emphasis could distort our perception of healthy lesbian and gay teens. Most such youth do manage to negotiate adolescence well with "creative resilience" (Kielwasser & Wolf, 1994, Footnote, p. 59).

2. Heterosexual histories are more common among females (Anderson, 1994).

3. Obviously, with such factors as coming out subsequent to childbirth, adoption, single parenthood, artificial insemination, shared parenting and the multitude of other possible arrangements, it is not necessary for lesbians or gays to forego parenthood, but they remain less likely than heterosexuals to become parents.

4. "The social worker should not practice, condone, facilitate or collaborate with any form of discrimination on the basis of race, color, sex, sexual orientation, age, religion, national origin, marital status, political belief, mental or physical handicap, or any other preference or personal characteristic, condition or status" (NASW, 1993, p. 5).

5. "The social worker should act to prevent and eliminate discrimination against any person on the basis of race, color, sex, sexual orientation, age, religion, national origin, marital status, political belief, mental or physical handicap, or any other preference or personal characteristic, condition or status" (NASW, 1993, p. 10).

REFERENCES

Anderson, D. (1994). Lesbian and gay adolescents: Social and developmental considerations. *High School Journal, 77*(1 & 2), 13-19.

Bell, A., & Weinberg, M. (1978). *Homosexualities*. New York: Simon & Schuster.

Berger, G., Hank, L., Rauzi, T., & Simkins, L. (1987). Detection of sexual orientation by heterosexuals and homosexuals. *Journal of Homosexuality, 13*(4), 83-100.

Berger, R., & Purchin, A. (1995). Gay and lesbian youth: A community mental health response. *Journal of Gay & Lesbian Social Services, 3*(4), 69-72.

Bieschke, K., & Matthews, C. (1996). Career counselor attitudes and behaviors toward gay, lesbian, and bisexual clients. *Journal of Vocational Behavior, 48,* 243-255.

Bloomfield, K. (1993). A comparison of alcohol consumption between lesbians and heterosexual women in an urban population. *Drug and Alcohol Dependence, 33,* 257-269.

D'Augelli, A., & Hershberger, S. (1993). Lesbian, gay and bisexual youth in community settings: Personal challenges and mental health problems. *American Journal of Community Psychology, 21*(4), 421-448.

Erwin, K. (1993). Interpreting the evidence: Competing paradigms and the emergence of lesbian and gay suicide as a "social fact." *International Journal of Health Services, 23*(3), 437-453.

Gibson, P. (1989). Gay male and lesbian youth suicide. *Report of the secretary's task force on youth suicide* (Alcohol, Drug Abuse and Mental Health Administration, DHHS Publication Number (ADM) 89-1623). (Volume 3: Prevention and interventions in youth suicide). Washington, DC: Superintendent of Documents, U.S. Government Printing Office.

Gonsiorek, J. (1991). The empirical basis for the demise of the illness model of homosexuality. In J. Gonsiorek & J. Weinrich (Eds.), *Homosexuality: Research implications for public policy* (pp. 115-136). Newbury Park, CA: Sage.

Hooker, E. (1957). The adjustment of the male overt homosexual. *Journal of Projective Techniques, 21*(1), 18-31.

Ivanoff, A., & Smyth, N. (1992). Intervening with suicidal individuals: Principles and guidelines for change. In K. Corcoran (Ed.), *Structuring change: Effective practice for common client problems* (pp. 111-137). Chicago: Lyceum Press.

Jay, K., & Young, A. (1979). *The gay report: Lesbians and gay men speak out about sexual experiences and lifestyles*. New York: Summit Books.

Kielwasser, A., & Wolf, M. (1994). Silence, difference and annihilation: Understanding the impact of mediated heterosexism on high school students. *High School Journal, 77*(1 & 2), 58-79.

Malyon, A. (1981). The homosexual adolescent: Developmental issues and social bias. *Child Welfare, 60*(5), 321-330.

Martin, A. D. (1982). Learning to hide: The socialization of the gay adolescent. *Adolescent Psychiatry, 10,* 52-65.

Morales, E. (1990). Ethnic minority families and minority gays and lesbians. *Marriage & Family Review, 14*(3/4), 217-239.

Morrow, D. (1993). Social work with gay and lesbian adolescents. *Social Work,* *38*(6), 655-660.

Muehrer, P. (1995). Suicide and sexual orientation: A critical summary of recent research and directions for future research. *Suicide & Life-Threatening Behavior, 25, Supplement,* 72-81.

Proctor, C., & Groze, V. (1994). Risk factors for suicide among gay, lesbian, and bisexual youths. *Social Work, 39*(5), 504-513.

Remafedi, G. (1990). Fundamental issues in the care of homosexual youth. *Medical Clinics of North America, 74*(5), 1169-1179.

Remafedi, G. (1994). *Death by denial: Studies of suicide in gay and lesbian teenagers.* Boston: Alyson.

Remafedi, G., Farrow, J., & Deisher, R. (1991). Risk factors for attempted suicide in gay and bisexual youth. *Pediatrics, 87,* 869-875.

Reynolds, A., & Koski, M. (1994). Lesbian, gay and bisexual teens and the school counselor: Building alliances. *High School Journal, 77*(1 & 2), 88-94.

Rittner, B., Smyth, N., & Wodarski, J. (1995). Assessment and crisis intervention strategies with suicidal adolescents. *Crisis Intervention, 2,* 71-84.

Robinson, K. (1991). Gay youth support groups: An opportunity for social work intervention. *Social Work, 36*(5), 458-459.

Saulnier, C. F., & Miller, B. (Under review). Childhood abuse as "explanation" of sexual orientation in women. [Available from author].

Savin-Williams, R. (1994). Verbal and physical abuse as stressors in the lives of lesbian, gay male, and bisexual youths: Associations with school problems, running away, substance abuse, prostitution and suicide. *Journal of Consulting and Clinical Psychology, 62*(2), 261-269.

Schneider, S., Farberow, N., & Kruks, G. (1989). Suicidal behavior in adolescent and young adult gay men. *Suicide and Life-Threatening Behavior, 19*(4), 381-394.

Singerline, H. (1994). OutRight: Reflections on an out-of school gay youth group. *High School Journal, 77*(1&2), 133-137.

Uribe, V. (1994). Project 10: A school-based outreach to gay and lesbian youth. *High School Journal, 77*(1 & 2), 108-112.

Vaid, U. (1995). *Virtual equality.* NY: Doubleday.

Vergara, T. (1984). Meeting the needs of sexual minority youth: One program's response. *Journal of Social Work & Human Sexuality, 2*(2/3), 19-38.

Wedded to the Status Quo: Same-Sex Marriage After *Baehr v. Lewin*

Sandra Kopels

In 1888, the Supreme Court of the United States described marriage as creating the most important relationship in life, having more to do with the morals and civilization of a people than any other institution (Maynard v. Hill). In 1923, the United States Supreme Court recognized that the right to marry, establish a home and bring up children is part of the liberty protected by the Due Process Clause of the Constitution (Meyer v. Nebraska). More recently, from a legal perspective, marriage has been viewed both as a fundamental right and a basic civil liberty, worthy of protection from governmental interference unless there are compelling reasons justifying such interference. Accordingly, laws which allowed the sterilization of habitual criminals (Skinner v. Oklahoma, 1942); laws which outlawed persons of different races from marrying each other (Loving v. Virginia, 1967); laws which interfered with a married couple's decision to receive

Sandra Kopels, JD, MSW, is Associate Professor, University of Illinois at Urbana, School of Social Work, 1207 W. Oregon, Urbana, IL 61801.

[Haworth co-indexing entry note]: "Wedded to the Status Quo: Same-Sex Marriage After *Baehr v. Lewin*." Kopels, Sandra. Co-published simultaneously in *Journal of Gay & Lesbian Social Services* (The Haworth Press, Inc.) Vol. 8, No. 3, 1998, pp. 69-81; and: *Violence and Social Injustice Against Lesbian, Gay and Bisexual People* (ed: Lacey M. Sloan, and Nora S. Gustavsson) The Haworth Press, Inc., 1998, pp. 69-81. Single or multiple copies of this article are available for a fee from The Haworth Document Delivery Service [1-800-342-9678, 9:00 a.m. - 5:00 p.m. (EST). E-mail address: getinfo@haworthpressinc.com].

information about birth control (Griswold v. Connecticut, 1965); and laws which prohibited persons with unpaid child support obligations from re-marrying (Zablocki v. Redhail, 1978) have all been struck down as uncon-stitutional infringements on individuals' fundamental rights to marriage and privacy within the marital relationship.

In addition to the recognized constitutional rights, marriage, as a legally sanctioned status, confers social and economic benefits and rights on those who enter into the marriage contract. These benefits include income tax advantages, such as deductions, credits, rates, and exemptions; gift and estate tax benefits; control, division, acquisition, and disposition of prop-erty as well as exemptions of property from attachment or execution; rights relating to dower, curtesy, and inheritance; child custody and sup-port awards; spousal support; premarital agreements; name changes; spou-sal testimonial privileges; wrongful death and loss of consortium actions; the ability to provide consent to emergency medical procedures; and em-ployee health, medical, and other benefits for spouses and children.

While marriage is clearly the traditionally favored social status, the right to marry is only available to persons who are members of opposite-sex couples. Marriage typically has been defined as the union between one man and one woman. Accordingly, the right to marry and the concomitant rights and benefits of marriage are unavailable to persons who are part of a same-sex relationship. Those involved in same-sex relationships often must resort to complicated, expensive, and time-consuming legal methods to obtain for themselves and their partners some of the incidental benefits of marriage. Therefore, by executing wills, contracts, trusts, or powers of attorney, property can be passed to partners at death and medical and financial decisions can be made by the partner in the case of incapacitation (Deitrich, 1994). Some gay and lesbian couples have tried to adopt their partners and others have used their municipality's domestic partnership arrangements to secure a form of legal status for their relationships. How-ever, there are limitations to the availability and effectiveness of these devices to imitate the status and benefits of marriage.

More than merely seeking financial and social benefits, lesbian and gay couples want recognition of their relationships as a means of validating their quality and importance as well as ending discrimination against homosexuality (Henson, 1994). By denying persons of the same-sex the right to marry, society views their commitment to each other as less worthy of public acceptance (Deitrich, 1994). If marriage were an option for homosexual relationships, the equalization of status with opposite sex couples would legitimize their relationships and go further to eradicate the deep-seated prejudice against homosexuals and their families than would any other type of legal reform (Henson, 1994).

This article reviews the recent court case of *Baehr v. Lewin* (1993) which ultimately may have the effect of legalizing same-sex marriages in Hawaii. While *Baehr* was neither the first nor last court case to attack a state statute which limited marriages to persons of the opposite-sex, it remains the only case that recognizes that such a prohibition may, in effect, be unconstitutional discrimination against same-sex couples on the basis of sex. Accordingly, it places the burden on the state to justify this discrimination. After reviewing the case and the legal bases for the court decision, this article will discuss specific aspects of the court's reasoning. Next, it will examine the impact of the decision and the legislative responses to the case. Finally, the article suggests that the status quo of prohibiting same-sex marriages will continue and that alternative solutions should be explored to obtain some form of legal recognition for same-sex relationships.

THE DECISION IN BAEHR V. LEWIN

In 1991, three same-sex couples (the Plaintiffs) sued John C. Lewin, in his official capacity as the Director of the State of Hawaii's Department of Health (DOH), for the Department's failure to issue marriage licenses to the Plaintiffs. Their complaint alleged that the DOH's interpretation and application of the Hawaii statute regarding marriage violated their rights to privacy and denied them due process and equal protection of the law, all of which were guaranteed under Hawaii's Constitution. Lewin's response asked for the Plaintiffs' case to be dismissed based on reasons including: (1) Hawaii's marriage laws view marriage as a union between a man and a woman; (2) the only legally recognizable marriages are heterosexual unions, therefore, the plaintiffs had no right to enter into state-licensed homosexual marriages; (3) the state's marriage laws did not interfere in any way with the Plaintiffs' private relationships; (4) the state is under no obligation to take affirmative steps to provide official approval to homosexual unions; (5) Hawaii's marriage laws protect, foster and may help perpetuate the basic family unit, vital to society, that provides status and a nurturing environment to children born to married persons and constitutes a statement of the moral values of the community; (6) homosexuals are not a protected class requiring heightened judicial scrutiny; and (7) Hawaii's marriage laws perform such a critical function in society and are so removed from burdening or interfering with the plaintiffs' private relationships that the laws must be sustained. After hearing arguments on the legal issues presented, the circuit court granted Lewin's motion to dismiss in October, 1991.

The Plaintiffs appealed to the Supreme Court of Hawaii, which found that the circuit court erred by making certain conclusions, as a matter of law, without a sufficient factual basis to support the conclusions. Specifically, the Hawaii Supreme Court ruled that the circuit court's order violated the Hawaii Constitution's equal protection clause. However, the Hawaii Supreme Court did not rule in favor of the Plaintiffs' due process and privacy claims.

The Plaintiffs had argued that the right to privacy in the Hawaii Constitution encompassed all of the fundamental rights guaranteed in the United States Constitution. Because the right to marry previously had been viewed by the United States Supreme Court as a fundamental right, protected by the due process clause, the Plaintiffs argued that the right to marry should be extended to same-sex couples. The U. S. Supreme Court had characterized the right to marriage as fundamental and on the same level of importance as decisions relating to procreation, childbirth, child rearing, and family relationships. The Hawaii court concluded that implicit in the Supreme Court's link between these rights was the assumption that the right to marry was the logical predicate of the other rights. In other words, the Hawaii court concluded that the federal construct of marriage, subsumed within the right to privacy, contemplates unions between men and women.

Therefore, the question presented to the Hawaii Supreme Court was whether it would create a *new* fundamental right–the right of same-sex couples to marry. Applying the traditional test to determine whether a right should be deemed fundamental, the Hawaii Supreme Court stated, "[W]e do not believe that a right to same-sex marriage is so rooted in the traditions and collective conscience of our people that failure to recognize it would violate the fundamental principles of liberty and justice that lie at the base of our civil and political institutions. Neither do we believe that a right to same-sex marriage is implicit in the concept of ordered liberty, such that neither liberty nor justice would exist if it were sacrificed . . . " (*Baehr* at 57). It concluded that the right to same-sex marriage was not a fundamental right arising out of the right to privacy or other sources.

Although the Hawaii Supreme Court denied the privacy and due process arguments, the Court stated that the Plaintiffs still retained a potential remedy by proceeding with their equal protection claims. Lewin had contended that homosexual partners cannot form a state licensed marriage, because marriage, as the term is defined and used, means a special relationship between a man and a woman. Therefore, individuals of the same sex cannot marry, not because of impermissible discrimination on the part of the State, but rather, because they have a biological inability to satisfy the definition of the status they desire. Lewin relied on previous cases which had determined that same-sex couples were ineligible to marry. In *Jones v. Hallahan* (1973), the Kentucky Supreme Court denied two women the right to marry, ruling that the women were prevented from marrying, not by the Kentucky statutes or by the refusal of the County Clerk to issue them a license, but because of their own "incapability" of entering into a marriage as that term is defined. In *Singer v. Hara* (1974), the Washington appellate court ruled that two men were denied the right to marry, not because they were discriminated against on the basis of their sex but instead, because of the nature of marriage itself.

The Court found Lewin's arguments unpersuasive and circular. Instead, it focused on Hawaii's Constitution which states that "[no] person shall . . . be denied the equal protection of the laws, nor be denied the enjoyment of the person's civil rights or be discriminated against in the exercise thereof because of race, religion, sex or ancestry." Equating the right to marry with a basic civil right, the Court stated that the Hawaii Constitution prohibits state-sanctioned discrimination against persons in the exercise of their civil right to marry on the basis of sex. The Court found that the Hawaii marriage statute, by its plain language and as applied by the DOH, restricted the marital relationship to a male and a female. Because the state regulated access to the status of married persons, on the basis of the sex of those who applied for a license, the Court viewed the marriage statute as establishing a sex-based classification. Accordingly, the equal protection clause of Hawaii's Constitution was implicated.

Once the Court determined that the equal protection clause was involved, it had to decide the level of judicial scrutiny it would apply. Significantly, the Hawaii Supreme Court held that sex is a "suspect category" for purposes of equal protection analysis under the Hawaii Constitution and is subject to the "strict scrutiny" test. The Hawaii Supreme Court held that the marriage statute which restricted marriage to a male and a female was presumed to be unconstitutional and sent the case back to the trial court to hear evidence. There, the burden would be on Lewin to show that "(a) the statute's sex-based classification is justified by compelling state interests and (b) the statute is narrowly drawn to avoid unnecessary abridgements of the applicant couple's constitutional rights" *(Baehr v. Lewin, 1993)*. The trial on these issues began in September 1996. In December 1996, Circuit Judge Kevin Chang ruled that the state had not met its burden and that the Hawaii marriage statute was unconstitutional.

DISCUSSION OF THE CASE

The determination that the Hawaii marriage statute infringed on the rights of a suspect class is of utmost importance to the ultimate outcome of the *Baehr* case. The lower court had ruled, as a matter of law, that homosexuals do not constitute a "suspect class" for purposes of equal protection analysis and therefore were not entitled to heightened judicial scrutiny. In contrast, the Hawaii Supreme Court viewed the marriage statute as involving sex-based discrimination rather than being connected to homosexuality. In fact, in a footnote to its decision, the Court stated that "homosexual" and "same-sex" marriages were not synonymous. Viewing homosexuality and heterosexuality as variants of sexual attraction, the Court said that parties to a union between "a man and a woman" may or may not be homosexuals and parties to a same-sex marriage could theoretically be either homosexuals or heterosexuals. By framing the statute as creating a sex-based classification, implicating the rights of members of a suspect class, the Court predetermined the level of scrutiny that would be applied to the marriage statute.

A suspect classification exists where the class of individuals formed by a statute, on its face or as administered, has been ". . . saddled with such disabilities, or subjected to such a history of purposeful unequal treatment or relegated to such a position of political powerlessness as to command extraordinary protection from the majoritarian political process" (*San Antonio v. Rodriguez,* 1973). The significance of the determination of a suspect class is that it subjects the statute to heightened and more rigorous judicial analysis (i.e., strict scrutiny) in which the underlying rationale for the classification has to implicate "compelling" state interests. When a suspect class is not involved, the rational basis test is used. Under that test, the inquiry is whether a statute rationally furthers a legitimate state interest. In other words, any reasonable justification for the legislative enactment is sufficient and the statute will be upheld.

Although the U.S. Supreme Court had previously ruled that sex based classifications merit an intermediate standard of judicial review, the Hawaii Court chose to apply the more stringent strict scrutiny test to gender classifications, equating sex with race, religion, and ancestry under Hawaii's Constitution. While proponents of homosexual rights can argue that homosexuals certainly fit the definition of a "suspect class" and that statutes should be highly scrutinized to assure governments have compelling state interests justifying the infringement of their rights, the law has not yet accepted this argument. In fact, at the time of the *Baehr* decision, the major U.S. Supreme Court ruling pertaining to homosexuality was *Bowers v. Hardwick* (1986), in which the Court ruled that homosexuals do not have the fundamental right to engage in sodomy. Most courts after *Bowers* have incorporated the antihomosexual rhetoric contained in the decision to conclude that homosexuals are not a suspect class (Hovermill, 1994). While the Supreme Court recently struck down Colorado's constitutional amendment which barred legislation protecting homosexuals from discrimination, the Court did not find homosexuals to be members of a suspect class (*Romer v. Evans*, 1996). Therefore, by characterizing the Hawaii marriage statute as gender-based discrimination, the Hawaii Supreme Court avoided judicial precedent which may have precluded application of the compelling state interest test.

COMPELLING STATE INTERESTS

When reviewing a statute that impacts upon the rights of a suspect class, the court subjects the legislation to a strict scrutiny standard of review that requires the law to be narrowly tailored to achieve a compelling state interest. The Court arrives at its determination by evaluating the classification itself, the importance of the governmental interests it seeks to achieve, and the closeness of the relationship between the classification and the objectives. The weight that the court gives these factors determines whether it believes the governmental interests are sufficiently "compelling."

A number of arguments have been advanced against same-sex marriages. These include: (1) the notion that marriage has always been considered by custom and by definition to be a union of a man and a woman; (2) homosexuality is immoral, therefore, same-sex marriages foster immorality; (3) consummation of a same-sex marriage would be the commission of sodomy which is a crime in many states; and (4) marriage uniquely involves the procreation and rearing of children within a family (D'Amato, 1995). One court stated that "marriage exists as a protected legal institution primarily because of societal values associated with the propagation of the human race. . . . no same-sex couple offers the possibility of the birth of children by their union. Thus the refusal of the state to authorize same-sex marriage results from such impossibility of reproduction rather than from an invidious discrimination on account of sex" (*Singer v. Hara*, 1974).

In the *Baehr* decision, the Hawaii Supreme Court sent the case back to the trial court to determine whether the State of Hawaii could demonstrate compelling state interests which were narrowly tailored to justify its ban on same-sex marriage. At the trial, which occurred in September 1996, Hawaii advanced as its primary reason for prohibiting same-sex marriages (one of its compelling state interests) the argument that children develop optimally in biological families; in a same-sex marriage at least one of the parents would not be a biological parent. Eight expert witnesses testified about child development issues and the need for children to develop good relationships with loving parents. Even the witnesses for the State, however, admitted that gays and lesbians raise children who were well-adjusted.

No one would dispute that the State has an interest in optimal child development. However, the reality of current social conditions results in children being raised in a multitude of family arrangements including single families, step families, adoptive families, and foster families. If the State of Hawaii prohibits same-sex marriages based on the belief that children's interests are best served in their biological families, it would logically follow that Hawaii should also prohibit heterosexual divorce and adoption of children.

In his December 1996 ruling, Justice Chang stated that while there certainly is a benefit to children from being raised by their mother and father in an intact home, the State of Hawaii had not proved that allowing same-sex marriages would result in significant differences in the development or outcomes of children raised by gay or lesbian parents as compared to children raised by their biological parents. Chang wrote, "Simply put, (the state) has failed to establish or prove that the public interest in the well-being of children and families, or the optimal development of children will be adversely affected by same-sex marriages." Moreover, he said that the state provided only "meager" evidence on the adverse effects same-sex marriage would have on the institution of marriage (Gay Marriages Upheld, 1996). Accordingly, because Hawaii could not provide a "compelling state interest" to justify the ban on same-sex marriages, prohibiting such marriages violated the equal protection clause of Hawaii's Constitution. However, Judge Chang entered an order which postponed enforcement of his ruling until the State's appeal is reviewed by the Hawaii Supreme Court.

IMPACT OF BAEHR V. LEWIN

Assuming that the Hawaii Supreme Court ultimately rules that the ban on same-sex marriage is unconstitutional, same-sex marriages will become legal in Hawaii. The question remains whether other states will honor same-sex marriages validly contracted in Hawaii and extend to the same-sex spouses the same rights and benefits of marriage enjoyed by heterosexual spouses. Therefore, if a same-sex couple were married in Hawaii and returned to another state to live, would the home state recognize the marriage? If the couple were to later divorce, would they have access to the court for resolution of the custody, property, and debt distribution issues? If an employer refused to allow the same-sex spouse's claim for health benefits under an insurance policy, would there be a means to redress this in the home state? From the judicial, legislative, and public reactions to the *Baehr* decision, it appears that same-sex marriages continue to be extremely disfavored and may become a phenomenon unique to Hawaii.

There is wide variation among state laws concerning marriage. States vary in the degree of kinship that can marry (e.g., first cousins), residency requirements, prerequisites to marriage, and the rights and obligations of the parties. The general rule of law is that a marriage which is validly contracted and recognized in the state where performed is valid everywhere. The ability of one state to reject a sister state's marriage law is limited by the Full Faith and Credit Clause of the Constitution which states that "Full Faith and Credit shall be given in each State to the public Acts, Records, and judicial Proceedings of every other State" (U.S. CONST. Art IV, § 1). In addition, when legal issues arise regarding the marriage, the law of the state in which the marriage was celebrated should be applied. By validating an out-of-state marriage and applying the law of the state where the marriage was performed, stability and predictability protect the expectations and interests of the parties. Theoretically, it would appear that if a same-sex couple chose to be married in Hawaii and then returned to their own state, the marriage would be legally recognized.

However, there are two closely related exceptions to the general rule of upholding valid, out-of-state marriages. If a state has a statute which clearly expresses that the general validation rule will not be applied or if a state has a strong public policy against recognizing a specific marriage, then the courts of that state will refuse to recognize a valid marriage from another state (Hovermill, 1994). Therefore, in the case of same-sex marriage, if a state has a statute that articulates that it would not recognize same-sex marriages or if same-sex marriages are clearly contrary to a state's strong public policy, that state would not recognize a valid same-sex marriage from Hawaii.

Prior to the *Baehr* decision, most state statutes were silent as to same-sex marriages. This is unsurprising because of the almost universally accepted belief that marriage is the union between a male and female. Because same-sex relationships were not contemplated to be within the definition of marriage, there would be little reason to enact a statutory provision to address this issue. In 1994, only three states expressly prohibited homosexual marriages (Hovermill, 1994). In 1995, five states had explicit requirements that couples seeking to marry be of the opposite sex (D'Amato, 1995). By fall 1996, 14 states had enacted bans on gay marriages while bills barring recognition of same-sex marriages had been introduced in 34 state legislatures ("Gay Activists," 1996).

The public policy of a state is expressed in its courts decisions, its constitution, and its legislation (Hovermill, 1994). No state's constitution mentions same-sex marriage and very few states have had court cases challenging the same-sex marriage issue. However, it appears that states are rushing to enact legislation to explicitly make clear their public policy regarding same-sex marriages within their borders. The effect of these statutory enactments is twofold: it not only prohibits same-sex marriages but also evinces strong public policy statements against such marriages. In this way, a same-sex couple would be unable to get married in their own state, nor would that state recognize their marriage even if it had been legally entered into and contracted in Hawaii.

States have taken a number of approaches in barring same-sex marriages and in expressing their public policies. For example, in Illinois, same-sex marriage was added to the list of prohibited marriages (Illinois Compiled Statutes Annotated, 1996). Until its addition, prohibited marriages only included relationships between certain relatives by blood or adoption. In Illinois, if a party enters into a legal marriage which is prohibited in Illinois although permitted elsewhere and then returns to live in Illinois, the marriage will not be recognized. By specifying same-sex marriage as a type of prohibited marriage which cannot be evaded by entering into it in another jurisdiction where legal, Illinois has provided an exception to the general rule of validation of out-of-state marriages. At the same time, the statute implies that same-sex marriages are against the public policy of Illinois.

South Carolina added a section to its law stating "a marriage between persons of the same sex is void *ab initio* and against the public policy of this State" (South Carolina Acts, 1996). By its express language, this statute makes explicit that same-sex marriage is against the public policy of South Carolina. In Georgia, a newly enacted law states, "No marriage between persons of the same sex shall be recognized as entitled to the benefits of marriage. Any marriage entered into by persons of the same-sex pursuant to a marriage license issued by another state. . . shall be void in this state. Any contractual rights granted . . . shall be unenforceable . . . and the courts . . . shall have no jurisdiction whatsoever under any circumstances . . . to grant a divorce or separate maintenance . . . or rule on any of the parties' respective rights . . ." (Official Code of Georgia Annotated, 1996). Through its express language, this statute makes it abundantly clear that Georgia will neither allow same-sex marriages nor allow its courts to be used under any circumstances to enforce the rights of persons who were validly married elsewhere. Ironically, even members of the Hawaii legislature are attempting to ban same-sex marriages by introducing legislation and a constitutional amendment before the compelling state interest issue is ruled on again by the Hawaii Supreme Court. In this way, the State of Hawaii would be able to demonstrate that their own public policy does not recognize same-sex marriages.

Fearing that same-sex marriages may become legal in Hawaii and that same-sex spouses may become entitled to federal benefits if legally married, the federal government recently passed legislation to "defend and protect the institution of marriage." The Defense of Marriage Act (P.L. 104-199), which became effective on September 21, 1996, defines "marriage" under federal law as "between one man and one woman as husband and wife" and "spouse" as "a person of the opposite sex who is a husband or wife." Under this law, benefits under a variety of federal programs, such as Social Security, federal income tax, Medicare, etc., are only available to persons who are properly defined as married spouses. Moreover, the Defense of Marriage Act provides that states are not required to give effect to legally sanctioned same-sex marriages from other states. For states that have not yet passed a law banning same-sex marriages, the Defense of Marriage Act grants federal authority for not following the Full Faith and Credit clause of the U.S. Constitution. For states that have passed a ban on same-sex marriage, the Defense of Marriage Act provides additional, federal public policy justifications for their ban.

CONCLUSION

From the perspective of changing the status quo, the impact of the *Baehr* decision can be viewed both positively and negatively. On the positive side, the *Baehr* court decided that prohibiting persons of the same sex from marrying is sex-based discrimination and placed the burden on the State of Hawaii to justify the discrimination. When the case was remanded to the trial court, Hawaii was unable to prove that denying same-sex marriages promotes optimal child development. Barring unforeseen constitutional or legislative changes, the Hawaii Supreme Court will almost certainly agree that the state had not met its burden of proof and had not demonstrated compelling state interests in prohibiting same-sex marriages. Accordingly, there will be no constitutional justification for banning same-sex marriages and same-sex couples will be allowed to marry in Hawaii.

On the negative side, it appears that the only state that may legalize same-sex marriage is Hawaii. After the *Baehr* decision, courts in New York and Washington, D.C. upheld state laws which limited marriage to males and females, rejecting the *Baehr* court's reasoning (*Storrs v. Holcomb*, 1996; *Dean v. D.C.*, 1995). The proliferation of state laws, which can be expected to continue, explicitly outlaws same-sex marriages. Formalizing the ban on same-sex marriage through explicit legislation has the effect of institutionalizing discrimination against homosexuals who desire to marry. Moreover, explicit legislation lends support to public policy arguments for non-recognition of same-sex marriages. Same-sex persons who legally marry in Hawaii and return to their home states may find it impossible to enforce the rights created by their marriage. While the variance among state laws invites continued litigation, the effect of the state prohibitions on same-sex marriage, coupled with the federal government's foray into the area, suggests that same-sex marriages will not be recognized, upheld, or enforced. In effect, the status quo will continue.

While the issues surrounding same-sex marriage will be debated through legislation and the courts, recognition of same-sex marriages and the rights of the persons who desire those marriages does not appear to be forthcoming. Accordingly, other strategies should be followed to attempt to secure some of the benefits and rights of marriage. One of these strategies is to pursue the creation of domestic partnership arrangements. Within the last year, Delaware, Hawaii, and California have introduced domestic or family partnership legislation to extend some benefits to same-sex couples, while preserving the "sanctity of marriage." Additionally, public and private industries can be lobbied to voluntarily extend employee benefits to same-sex partners. At the same time the same-sex marriage case was being tried in Hawaii, as a way of providing equity to their employees, IBM announced that it had decided to grant benefits to gay and lesbian live-in partners. Another legislative strategy is to pursue anti-discrimination laws against homosexuals, especially in the workplace. On the same day that Congress overwhelmingly passed the Defense of Marriage Act, a law which guaranteed non-discrimination against homosexuals in the workplace was very narrowly defeated. While the country may not be ready to extend the right to marry to same-sex couples, there is a growing acceptance that workplace discrimination against homosexuals should not be tolerated. As perceptions of homosexuals change, then other rights may also be extended to them.

When a Milwaukee legislator announced that she was going to introduce legislation to legalize same-sex marriages in Wisconsin, the proposal was called a "social reign of terror" and equated with "inner-city violence, drugs and crime" as destroyers of the traditional family (Dietrich, 1994). Clearly, society does not appear ready to extend the basic civil right to marry to homosexuals. Despite the possible legalization of same-sex marriage in Hawaii, for the present time, the status quo will likely continue.

REFERENCES

Baehr v. Lewin, 852 P. 2d 44 (1993).

Bowers v. Hardwick, 478 U.S. 186 (1986).

D'Amato, A.D. (1995). Conflict of law rules and the interstate recognition of same-sex marriages. *University of Illinois Law Review, 1995*, 911-943.

Dean v. D.C., 653 A.2d. 307 (D.C. 1995).

Dietrich, J. (1994). The lessons of the law: Same-sex marriage and *Baehr v. Lewin. Marquette Law Review, 78*, 121-152.

Gay activists vow to keep up marriage fight. (1996, September 11). *Honolulu Star-Bulletin*, p. 6.

Gay marriages upheld. (1996, December 4). *The Honolulu Advertiser*, p. A6.

Griswold v. Connecticut, 381 U.S. 479 (1965).

Henson, D. (1994). Will same-sex marriages be recognized in sister states?: Full faith and credit and due process limitations on states' choice of law regarding the status and incidents of homosexual marriages following Hawaii's Baehr v. Lewin. *University of Louisville Journal of Family Law, 32*(3), 551-600.

Hovermill, J.W. (1994). A conflict of laws and morals: The choice of law implications of Hawaii's recognition of same-sex marriages. *Maryland Law Review, 53*, 450-493.

Illinois Compiled Statutes Annotated, 750 ILCS 5/212 (1996).

Jones v. Hallahan, 510 S.W. 2d 588 (Ky. Ct. App. 1973).

Loving v. Virginia, 388 U.S. 1 (1967).

Maynard v. Hill, 125 U.S. 190 (1888).

Meyer v. Nebraska, 262 U.S. 390 (1923).

Official Code of Georgia Annotated, §19-3-3.1 (1996).

Romer v. Evans, ___U.S.___, 116 S. Ct. 1620 (1996).

San Antonio Independent School District v. Rodriguez, 411 U.S. 1 (1973).

Singer v. Hara, 11 Wash. App. 247, 522 P. 2d 1187 (1974).

Skinner v. Oklahoma, 316 U.S. 535 (1942).

South Carolina Acts, 1996 S. C. Acts 327, §20-1-15 (1996).

Storrs v. Holcomb, 645 N.Y.S. 2d 286 (1996).

Zablocki v. Redhail, 434 U.S. 374 (1978).

Working Against Discrimination: Gay, Lesbian and Bisexual People on the Job

Jeane W. Anastas

SUMMARY. Gay, lesbian, and bisexual people may encounter problems in gaining employment or promotion, being ensured safe working conditions, and obtaining equitable earnings and benefits. Discrimination based on sexual orientation is not forbidden in most states, localities and employing organizations. Practice with gay, lesbian, and bisexual people must address work-related issues at personal, interpersonal, organizational, and policy levels. *[Article copies available for a fee from The Haworth Document Delivery Service: 1-800-342-9678. E-mail address: getinfo@haworthpressinc.com]*

To love and to work are essential to human functioning. Gay, lesbian and bisexual people are usually thought about in relation to how they love. However, gay, lesbian and bisexual people also work; that is, they participate in the paid labor force, most likely at higher rates than heterosexual people do (Morgan & Brown, 1991; Elliott, 1993; Fassinger, 1995). Participating in employment, being ensured safe working conditions, and sharing equitably in earnings and benefits are fundamental aspects of human rights. Work is essential to the economic well-being of individuals, households and families. In addition, working is a major way in which

Jeane W. Anastas, PhD, MSW, is affiliated with Smith College School for Social Work, Lilly Hall, Northhampton, MA 01063.

[Haworth co-indexing entry note]: "Working Against Discrimination: Gay, Lesbian and Bisexual People on the Job." Anastas, Jeane W. Co-published simultaneously in *Journal of Gay & Lesbian Social Services* (The Haworth Press, Inc.) Vol. 8, No. 3, 1998, pp. 83-98; and: *Violence and Social Injustice Against Lesbian, Gay and Bisexual People* (ed: Lacey M. Sloan, and Nora S. Gustavsson) The Haworth Press, Inc., 1998, pp. 83-98. Single or multiple copies of this article are available for a fee from The Haworth Document Delivery Service [1-800-342-9678, 9:00 a.m. - 5:00 p.m. (EST). E-mail address: getinfo@haworthpressinc.com].

people develop and express their individual talents and aptitudes, contributing to society as a whole as well as to their own self-maintenance (Poverny & Finch, 1988).

An ecological perspective on violence emphasizes the variety of forms violence takes, from the interpersonal to the social, cultural and economic. Discrimination against gay, lesbian and bisexual people in employment is a form of violence that denies them full participation in essential social and economic activities and institutions, perpetuates economic injustice, and reduces their opportunities for fulfilling human potential. Homophobia and heterosexism are forms of oppression that affect personal, interpersonal and institutional behavior (Appleby & Anastas, 1997, forthcoming). They form the context in which gay, lesbian, and bisexual people live out all aspects of their lives, including their work lives. Gay, lesbian and bisexual people ". . . have an overall potential to contribute to society similar to that of heterosexual people, including in the workplace" (Melton, 1989, p. 936). Homophobia and heterosexism in the workplace do violence to the gay, lesbian and bisexual people directly affected as well as to their families and communities.

This paper will summarize what is currently known about the employment problems of gay, lesbian, and bisexual people and suggest what the social work response should be. The emphasis will be on lesbian and gay workers, although bisexual people who are not married, who seek work-related benefits for a same-gender partner, or who openly identify as bisexual may encounter the same forms of discrimination at work that gay and lesbian people do. Unfortunately, almost all of the information available about discrimination against gay, lesbian, and bisexual people at work is based on whites of European descent, which is a serious limitation in our knowledge base.

FORMS OF WORKPLACE DISCRIMINATION

Gay or lesbian people may not be hired or may be fired from a job simply because of their sexual orientation (Badgett, 1996; Elliott, 1993; Friskopp & Silverstein, 1995; Poverny & Finch, 1988; Terry, 1992; Woods, 1993).[1] For example, in one well-publicized instance, in 1991 a roadside restaurant chain in the South and Midwest fired all of its known gay, lesbian, and bisexual employees because "they failed to demonstrate

---

1. Most of the studies on which these conclusions are based did not ask about or sample bisexual people.

normal heterosexual values" (Elliott, 1993, p. 217), an order that was later rescinded due to picketing and protest by gay and lesbian activists and their friends and family members. Self-report surveys suggest that between 16 and 44 percent of gay and lesbian people have encountered discrimination in employment or promotion because of their sexual orientation (Woods, 1993). Thus, even those gay, lesbian, and bisexual people who are employed worry about a "lavender ceiling" that may prevent them from reaching their full potential on the job (Friskopp & Silverstein, 1995).

Basic employment protection for lesbian, gay and/or bisexual workers is guaranteed by law in only a few states, counties and localities, although the number is gradually increasing. Although public opinion surveys show that people oppose discrimination against gay, lesbian, and bisexual people at work (Ellis, 1996), in 1996 proposed federal legislation to guarantee fair employment for gay, lesbian, or bisexual people was defeated. Employers themselves vary widely in their stated policies toward lesbian, gay, and bisexual workers (Elliott, 1993). Some state explicitly that they do not discriminate on the basis of sexual orientation. Some state that they make employment decisions strictly on ability and performance, not addressing or not inquiring about sexual orientation (resembling the "don't ask, don't tell" policy currently used in the United States military), what Woods (1993) has termed the "asexual imperative." Others openly state that they do take action based on sexual orientation in a variety of ways "when sexual orientation interferes with job performance, disrupts other employees or adversely affects the company" (Elliott, 1993, p. 217). As Woods (1993) notes in his study of gay men in corporate employment, the argument that sexual orientation is "disruptive" in the workplace ". . . is a brutal, circular form of prejudice: A gay man's sexuality is disruptive because others despise him for it" (p. 244). Some employers simply state that they will do only what local, state, or federal law requires of them. In general, public employees may more often be protected from discrimination than those in the private sector (Badgett, 1996).

Contrary to the stereotype and given the gender segmentation of the labor market, most gay men, lesbians, and bisexual people work in jobs that are typical for their genders. That is, most gay men work in "masculine" jobs, and most lesbians work in "feminine" ones (Kitzinger, 1991; Woods, 1993). In addition, even when gay men or lesbians do aspire to stereoptypically "gay" or non-traditional occupations for their gender, their aspirations in relation to status and prestige are no different from those of heterosexuals (Chung, 1995). However, it is not known how and to what degree a gay, lesbian, or bisexual orientation generally affects occupational choice (Ellis, 1996).

There are some professions and occupations in which gay, lesbian, or bisexual workers are more likely to encounter homophobia than in others. Although there is no evidence that a same-gender sexual orientation is caused by interpersonal influences in early life, educators at all levels, but especially those who work with young children, may be confronted with fears that they will influence impressionable children and youth to become lesbian or gay or that they may seduce or molest them (Fassinger, 1993; Kitzinger, 1991). Where local policy or legislation specifically forbids presenting "positive images of homosexuality" in the classroom, pressures on gay, lesbian and bisexual teachers can be especially intense (Kitzinger, 1991). Physicians, especially pediatricians, may also encounter problems (Fassinger, 1993; Fikar, 1992; Parker, 1994). For different reasons, gay and lesbian people may encounter problems in the military and in the clergy, although it should be noted that religious organizations and denominations vary widely in their attitudes and practices related to gay and lesbian clerics (Anderson & Smith, 1993; Chung, 1995; McSpadden, 1993).

Harassment on the Job

Whether or not lesbian, gay, and bisexual people openly identify as such at work, they may well face personal anti-gay attack. One extreme of the continuum of expression of anti-gay attitudes at work is overt harassment, threats, intimidation, and assault (Friskopp & Silverstein, 1995; Kitzinger, 1991; McNaught, 1993; Rosabal, 1996). At the other end of the continuum are bathroom graffiti, the anti-gay cartoon taped to an office door, or the joke told at the lunchroom table (Friskopp & Silverstein, 1995; McNaught, 1993). Miller (1995) has observed that the "corporate definition of competency" is of a white married (with children) male (p. 15). All of these forms of harassment on the job underscore how gay, lesbian, and bisexual people depart from this norm, and they have a corrosive effect, both personally and as workers. A gay, lesbian, or bisexual worker of color must often decide when making a complaint whether the incident is based on race or sexual orientation. In general, there is evidence that lesbians and gay men of color are at increased risk of victimization because of sexual orientation (Rosabel, 1996). Anti-discrimination policies that include sexual orientation are the best tool for combatting these forms of harassment, especially when coupled with company-wide employee diversity training that includes sexual orientation issues (McNaught, 1993, Poverny & Finch, 1988; Woods, 1993).

Employment Benefits

A major focus of anti-discriminatory policies in the workplace must be the heterosexist bias that defines fringe benefits packages, especially the definitions of "family" used both in law and in company and insurance policies (Poverny & Finch, 1988; Seck, Finch, Mor-Barak, & Poverny, 1933; Spielman & Winfeld, 1996). Domestic partnerships and co-parenting relationships must be recognized not only in health and dental care but also in child and other dependent care benefits and in pension, insurance and other survivors' rights (Spielman & Winfeld, 1996; Seck et al., 1993). Not only are benefits denied to the children and partners affected; when the value of employee benefits is added to the value of wages, for gay, lesbian and bisexual workers ". . . the result is total compensation lower than that of married co-workers performing the same job" (Eblin, 1990). In 1996, more than 60 corporations and public agencies, at least 30 colleges, universities and professional schools, and about 20 not-for-profit organizations in the United States were offering employee benefits to domestic partners (Zuckerman & Simons, 1996).

Most of the objections to and fears about including domestic partnerships in employment benefit packages have been found to have little basis in fact. The first objection is usually cost, and employee benefits as a whole do indeed represent a significant proportion of payroll costs. However, fears that domestic partnership benefits and/or claims might be more costly than those accorded to married couples have proven to be unfounded (Eblin, 1990; Spielman & Winfeld, 1996). Domestic partnerships have been well-defined in the local law and regulation (McNaught, 1993; Spielman & Winfeld, 1996). Recognizing domestic partnerships for same-gender relationships reduces the current inequity in total compensation for gay, lesbian and bisexual employees.

Differences Between Gay Men and Lesbians

To the extent that heterosexism and homophobia are the basis for workplace discrimination, lesbians and gay men may encounter similar problems at work. However, there are also ways in which anti-gay prejudices and workplace problems may be manifested differently for men and women (Friskopp & Silverstein, 1995). It has long been acknowledged that women in general are at a disadvantage in the world of work. Lesbians and bisexual women thus are likely to encounter gender discrimination on the job–in hiring, compensation, benefits, and advancement. This gender discrimination can occur along with or apart from discrimination issues related to sexual orientation (Badgett, 1996; Elliott, 1993; Fassinger, 1995;

Friskopp & Silverstein, 1995; Schneider, 1987). As a result, lesbians typically earn less than gay men (Badgett, 1996; Elliott, 1993). In addition, because lesbians are more likely to designate themselves as the head of a household than gay men are (Elliott, 1993), exclusion of domestic partnerships from employment benefits and limitations on ways to claim a child as a dependent (as in the case of a partner's child not related by biology or adoption to the employee) more often affect lesbians than gay men. Surveys suggest that lesbians may be less likely than gay men to be "out" at work, perhaps because of their concerns about gender discrimination (Badgett, 1996).

There is some evidence that lesbian workers may be more likely than heterosexual women to define and to condemn unwanted sexual remarks and advances at work as sexual harassment than heterosexual women do (Schneider, 1982). In addition, there is one form of sexual harassment particular to lesbians at work (and elsewhere): sexual harassment or assault by men designed to impose heterosexual sex upon them because they are lesbians (Kitzinger, 1991). Although most lesbians, like most other women, work in stereotypically "feminine" jobs, women, including lesbians, in nontraditional work roles face higher levels of harassment on the job, often harassment that specifically targets their sexual orientation. For example, media accounts show that women athletes in tennis and golf are often suspected of being lesbians, and those who do come out as lesbians have been accused of discrediting their sport. As another example, women in the military are discharged because of their sexual orientation much more often than men, in part because of the sexism that views military service as inherently and properly "masculine" (Anderson & Smith, 1993). Lesbians in all kinds of work roles, therefore, may take pains to appear quite "feminine" as a method of avoiding disclosure of their lesbianism or as a way to avoid harassment based on sexual orientation. However, one study suggests that lesbians who are more open about their sexual orientation may actually experience fewer incidents of sexual harassment than those who are less open because most workplace sexual harassment is based on the idea that a woman is heterosexually available (Schneider, 1982).

Gay men also may face forms of discrimination at work particular to them. Gay men are still associated in many people's minds with HIV and AIDS; thus gay men at work may encounter irrational fears and even harassment based on their assumed HIV status (Poverny & Finch, 1988; McNaught, 1988), a problem much less likely to be encountered by lesbians. Few employers have written policies about AIDS, and, although the Americans with Disabilities Act forbids discrimination against persons with AIDS, many such instances indeed occur (Miller, 1995; Roth & Carman, 1993).

Gay men in occupations considered quintessentially masculine, most notably the military (Anderson & Smith, 1993) and professional sports (Barret, 1993), may be subject to particularly intense harassment and may take extraordinary measures to keep their sexual orientation hidden. The fact that these occupations regularly bring men together in all-male living and/or bathing situations may make the gay male especially threatening to co-workers, leading, for example, to the argument that gay men in the military inevitably harm "combat effectiveness" by disrupting "morale, discipline and good order" (Anderson & Smith, 1993, p. 70). Since sexual orientation *per se* has been shown not to affect job performance, even in the military, the goal must be to eliminate such discrimination wherever it occurs.

Gay and Lesbian Workers of Color

As has already been mentioned, very little is known about gay, lesbian, and bisexual workers of color. In general, a non-majority racial or ethnic identity and a lesbian, gay, or bisexual one are not simply additive; they interact in complex gender- and culture-specific ways (Appleby & Anastas, forthcoming; deMonteflores, 1993; Rosabal, 1996). Because so little is known about them, Friskopp and Silverstein's (1995) study of lesbian and gay graduates of the Harvard Business School oversampled respondents of color. In general, those they interviewed considered that they were at risk of multiple discrimination, although their race was more often a problem to them than their sexual orientation largely because the latter aspect of their identities could often be successfully concealed. Moreover, being gay or lesbian sometimes compromised their ability to draw support outside of the workplace from their racial or ethnic communities, and being a person of color sometimes limited the support available in the gay or lesbian community. Some in this highly privileged group of workers, however, viewed their ability to use both of these networks and potential sources of support as an asset.

Transsexual and Other Transgendered People

Problems at the point of hiring may be even more acute for transsexual people than it is for gay, lesbian, and bisexual people. For example, the request to produce a birth certificate may call into question the gender designation (male or female) on an employment application, especially for someone who has not undergone a surgical gender reassignment process, after which such documents are legally altered in some countries (Kitzinger, 1991). Prior to gender reassignment surgery, transsexual people are required to live for at least a year as a member of the gender they feel themselves to be, and some transsexual people do not elect to have surgery but simply make the change medically and/or socially. However, their transsexual adjustment includes such practices at work as using the restroom for the gender they will become but which they do not yet anatomically "match." In other cases, an employee may undergo the social and/or surgical gender reassignment process while an ongoing employee. In such a case, human resource and other appropriate personnel must be prepared to ensure the individual safety in the workplace and to provide education and support to co-workers who may be confused by and lack information about the process (McNaught, 1993). Only those transgendered but not transsexual individuals who can feel emotionally comfortable only when they cross-dress completely on a daily basis present a pressing problem to most employers (McNaught, 1993).

COPING WITH DISCRIMINATION

The strategies that gay, lesbian, and bisexual people use to avoid or cope with employment discrimination may affect their job opportunities. Gays and lesbians, especially those who are more public in their self-identification, may develop or seek out self-employment opportunities for greater comfort in their work lives. Because gay and lesbian people may choose to settle in communities that provide an identifiable gay community, a protective civil rights environment, and/or enhanced employment and social opportunities (Chung, 1995; Hetherington, Hillerbrand & Etringer, 1989), over time career advancement may be limited by lack of geographic mobility (Elliott, 1993). Partner relocation may also be an issue (Hetherington et al., 1989; Friskopp & Silverstein, 1995; Hillerbrand & Orzek, 1989). Thus, like members of other minority groups, gay, lesbian, and bisexual workers ". . . may reach a plateau far too early in their careers" (Seck et al., 1993, p. 67). Many of the coping strategies gay, lesbian, and bisexual workers employ center around identity management, that is, around coming out (Pope, 1996).

One result of heterosexism and homophobia is the assumption of heterosexuality; that is, no one is assumed to be gay, lesbian, or bisexual in the absence of specific social cues or information to that effect. While the assumption of heterosexuality may be statistically correct, it creates many social and personal strains and difficulties at work for those who do not fit it. Whatever the coping strategy, the result is often a feeling of social marginalization and interpersonal stress (Badgett, 1996; Chung, 1995; Poverny & Finch, 1988; Powers, 1996).

Coming Out at Work

Whether to "come out," that is, to reveal a lesbian, gay, or bisexual identity to a supervisor or co-worker, is a major preoccupation of lesbian, gay, or bisexual workers (Ellis, 1996). Many gay, lesbian, and bisexual people who have come out in their private lives are not "out" at work, believing many aspects of private life, especially sexuality, to be irrelevant in that setting (Woods, 1993). However, the strains associated with active or passive concealment are considerable. As Hall has described it for lesbians:

> All the forms of non-disclosure, whether the occasional substitute of "he" or "she" when describing a week-end outing with a lover or the complete fabrication of a heterosexual life, leave a lesbian in a morally untenable position. Not only is she lying . . . she is ignoring the strong exhortations of the lesbian community to come out. (Hall, 1986, p. 73)

Currently, the relationship between coming out and job and employment consequences is poorly understood (Badgett, 1996).

Coming out is never a one-time event; as clients or customers, co-workers and supervisors change over time, the decision about what to say or not say about a lesbian, gay or bisexual identity must be continually made and remade (Fassinger, 1995; Friskopp & Silverstein, 1995; Griffin & Zuckas, 1993; Hall, 1986; Kitzinger, 1991; Pope, 1996). Moreover, the self-identification can be made directly or indirectly. An employee may actively hide a gay or lesbian orientation, such as by bringing a "date" of the opposite gender to work-related social events; conversely, an employee may openly announce a lesbian, gay or bisexual identity and/or bring a same-gender partner to such events. In between is the strategy of not concealing the facts of one's life, even to the extent of speaking up for gay rights in the work context, but also not definitely declaring a gay, lesbian or bisexual identity. Thus lesbian, gay and bisexual workers are often in some intermediate or "borderline" state of knowing that some people at work know about their sexual orientation while being uncertain about what others do or do not know or assume about them (Friskopp & Silverstein, 1995; Griffin & Zuckas, 1993; Kitzinger, 1991). This uncertainty also leads to difficulties in interpreting workplace events; if one is snubbed in the lunchroom or overlooked for a promotion, it is especially difficult to determine whether anti-gay prejudice is a factor if it is uncertain as to whether the fact itself is known or understood (Gonsiorek, 1993). Finally, there is the possibility that a gay or lesbian worker's sexual orientation will be revealed at work involuntarily, that is, through "outing" by others, often with painful negative consequences (Badgett, 1996).

One recent study suggested that openness about a lesbian or gay orientation at work was correlated with job and life satisfaction; that is, those survey respondents who were open with both co-workers and supervisors had generally higher levels of job satisfaction (Ellis & Riggle, 1995). However, those who were less open were more satisfied with their pay and had marginally higher salaries. Job satisfaction was also higher when the employer had a non-discrimination policy. Because the sample in this study was drawn from two cities, one with and one without a city ordinance protecting gay civil rights, the effect of this difference in locale was also examined. Workers who lived in the city with civil rights protection were more likely to report that their employers had anti-discrimination policies that protected lesbian, gay, and bisexual workers than those who did not. In addition, those in the city with civil rights protection were more likely to be open about their sexual orientation at work and to have higher levels of life satisfaction when *more* open; however, those in the city without civil rights protection had higher levels of life satisfaction when they were *less* open on the job. Thus, not surprisingly, both employees and employers were shown to be very sensitive to the environment in which they worked (Badgett, 1996; Fassinger, 1995; Friskopp & Silverstein, 1995; Schneider, 1987).

Decisions about coming out at work (and elsewhere) are not decisions that a gay, lesbian, or bisexual worker makes in a vacuum. Those who are in stable couple relationships must also consider the other member of the couple, whose own employment situation may be similar or different in its tolerance or safety level. Often, then, there are two sets of decisions to be made about identity management in two usually different work situations. Issues of being out on the job can be confounded with issues of commitment to the relationship, especially if members of the couple handle their sexual identity differently at work (Fassinger, 1995; Morgan & Brown, 1991).

Revealing one's sexual orientation on the job is distinct from deciding to become vocationally concerned with gay, lesbian, and bisexual rights or issues (Pope, 1996). In a study of academic sociologists, being active on sexual orientation issues–politically or as a focus of scholarship–as opposed to simply being open about one's sexual orientation was correlated with reports of negative career consequences, including job discrimination in hiring, promotion, and even harassment and intimidation (Taylor & Raeburn, 1995). However, in an intensive study of male and female schoolteachers in the Netherlands, gay men and lesbians adopted different strategies of self-presentation in the school setting. More (but not all) of the gay men were overtly or behaviorally "out," and some of them also saw themselves as actively engaged in political struggle for gay rights in the workplace. The lesbians more often concerned themselves with issues of gender equity in the setting rather than with sexual orientation issues in the workplace and saw themselves as responding to the needs of students and/or of the work group as a whole rather than as pursuing personal concerns (Dankmeijer, 1993). The author concluded that ". . . coming out fitted the lifestyle only of those who took on the role of crusaders for gay liberation" (p. 95). These studies highlight the variability in style and behavior, even among lesbian and bisexual people who self-identify as such at work and the consequences that may follow from the different identity management strategies employed.

IMPLICATIONS FOR SOCIAL WORK

Because work is so central to self-maintenance and self-esteem as well as to meaning in life, practice with lesbian, gay, and bisexual people that recognizes both the importance of work and the special problems that gay, lesbian, and bisexual workers may encounter as workers is a major way to contribute to the well-being of lesbian, gay, and bisexual people (Elliott, 1993; Morgan & Brown, 1991; Poverny & Finch, 1988). However, theories about work and career development, even those that have been adapted to women and their work, have not yet been systematically applied to lesbian, gay, or bisexual workers (Morgan & Brown, 1991; Pope, 1966). Thus there is little specific knowledge to guide the practitioner in dealing with issues related to work. However, those who work in Employee Assistance Programs (EAPs) or whose practice focusses specifically on issues of employment and training have an especially important role to play (Poverny & Finch, 1988; VanDenBergh, 1994).

People engaged in career and employment counseling must be educated about and trained in handling lesbian and gay issues and about heterosexism and homophobia and their effects (Elliott, 1993; Fassinger, 1995; Hetherington, Hillerbrand, & Etringer, 1989; Hetherington & Orzek, 1989; Morgan & Brown, 1991, Poverny & Finch, 1988; Prince, 1995; VanDenBergh, 1994). They cannot afford to make the assumption that all their clients are heterosexual. They must also be aware that sexual orientation can affect educational and occupational decision-making and can complicate career development and advancement (Pope, 1996). Identity management issues can be more intense at work or can be handled quite differently than in other aspects of a client's life. Helping a client to appraise work-related situations–to decide whether discrimination or social marginalization have occurred and to decide how to respond–is often important, especially when the client is in an intermediate state of openness on the job. Practitioners must therefore be aware of the facts about workplace discrimination and about the provisions, if any, that may protect the rights of a lesbian, gay, or bisexual worker in his or her locale or work organization.

Because of the many forms heterosexism and homophobia take in the workplace, efforts must include action on a variety of levels (Poverny & Finch, 1988). One corporate consultant has summarized them as follows:

1. an explicit employment policy that prohibits discrimination based on sexual orientation;
2. creation of a safe work environment that is free of heterosexist, homophobic and AIDSphobic behavior;
3. company-wide education about gay issues in the workplace and about AIDS;
4. an equitable benefits program that recognizes the [children and] domestic partners of gay, lesbian and bisexual employees;
5. support of a gay/lesbian/bisexual employee support group;
6. freedom for all employees to participate fully in all aspects of corporate life;
7. public support of gay issues. (McNaught, 1993, p. 66)

Regarding gay, lesbian, and bisexual workers as members of a nonethnic cultural minority group suggests that gay and lesbian issues be included in all diversity training and anti-discrimination efforts (Elliot, 1993; Hetherington et al., 1989; Hetherington & Orzek, 1989; Poverny & Finch, 1988; Powers, 1996). Support of broader social and public policy efforts to eliminate all forms of violence and discrimination against gay, lesbian, and bisexual people is essential in the effort since both work organizations and individual workers are very sensitive and responsive to the general legal and policy climates in which they function.

Finally, it should be noted that social work itself is not free of anti-gay prejudice and discrimination. While there has to date been no large-scale study of the work experiences of lesbian, gay, and bisexual social workers, there are major differences in views on gay and lesbian civil rights within the profession, even though one view predominates in its public documents (Van Soest, 1996). The recently revised social policy statement of NASW on gay, lesbian, and bisexual issues states:

> Prejudice toward lesbian, gay, and bisexual social workers results in discriminatory personnel practices and unnecessary stress. It should be noted that even within the profession, lesbian, gay, and bisexual social workers do not necessarily feel safe to openly and publicly declare their sexual orientation. It is imperative, therefore, that all social workers examine their attitudes and feelings about homosexuality and their understanding of lesbian, gay and bisexual cultures and work toward full social and legal acceptance of lesbian, gay and bisexual people. Ongoing self-examination will ensure that social workers remain aware of the negative impact that prejudice and discrimination have on their lesbian, gay, and bisexual clients and colleagues and can minimize homophobic responses that may arise in treatment or professional settings. (National Association of Social Workers, 1997)

Because of statutes in some states that criminalize the sexual behaviors that are common in same-gender sex (Badgett, 1996) and because of the "moral character" aspects of state-based licensing and credentialing, social workers' openness about a lesbian, gay, or bisexual identity may be inhibited, especially if the state lacks, as most do, basic civil rights protection for gay, lesbian, and bisexual people. Most important, gay, lesbian, and bisexual clients will only feel as safe and comfortable in the social work relationship as well as on the job as gay, lesbian and bisexual social workers themselves do.

REFERENCES

Anderson, C. W., & Smith, H. R. (1993). Stigma and honor: Gay, lesbian and bisexual people in the U.S. military. In L. Diamant (Ed.), *Homosexual issues in the workplace* (pp. 65-89). Washington, DC: Taylor & Francis.
Appleby, G. A., & Anastas, J. W. (forthcoming). *Not just a passing phase: Social work with gay, lesbian and bisexual people.* New York: Columbia University Press.
Appleby, G. A., & Anastas, J. W. (1998). Social work practice with lesbian, gay and bisexual people. In A. T. Morales & B. W. Sheafor, *Social work: A profession of many faces (8th ed.).* (pp. 313-345). Boston: Allyn & Bacon.
Badgett, M. V. L. (1996). Employment and sexual orientation: Disclosure and discrimination in the workplace. *Journal of Gay & Lesbian Social Services,* 4(4), 29-52.

Barret, R. L. (1993). The homosexual athlete. In L. Diamant (Ed.), *Homosexual issues in the workplace* (pp. 161-178). Washington, DC: Taylor & Francis.

Chung, Y. B. (1995). Career decision making of lesbian, gay and bisexual individuals. *The Career Development Quarterly, 44,* 178-190.

Dankmeijer, R. (1993). The construction of identities as a means of survival: Case of gay and lesbian teachers. *Journal of Homosexuality, 24*(3/4), 95-105.

deMontefiores, C. (1993). Notes on the management of difference. In Garnets, L. D., & Kimmel, D. C. (Eds.), *Psychological perspectives on lesbian and gay male experience* (pp. 218-247). NY: Columbia University Press.

Eblin, R. L. (1990). Domestic partnership recognition in the workplace: Equitable employee benefits for gay couples (and others). *Ohio State Law Journal, 51*(4), 1067-1087.

Elliott, J. E. (1993). Career development with lesbian and gay clients. *The Career Development Quarterly, 41*(3), 210-226.

Ellis, A. L. (1996). Sexual identity issues in the workplace: Past and present. *Journal of Gay & Lesbian Social Services, 4*(4), 1-16.

Ellis, A. L., & Riggle, E. D. D. (1995). The relation of job satisfaction and degree of openness about one's sexual orientation for lesbians and gay men. *Journal of Homosexuality, 30*(2), 75-85.

Fassinger, R. E. (1993). And gladly teach: Lesbian and gay issues in education. In L. Diamant (Ed.), *Homosexual issues in the workplace* (pp. 119-142). Washington, DC: Taylor & Francis.

Fassinger, R. E. (1995). From invisibility to integration: Lesbian identity in the workplace. *Career Development Quarterly, 44*(2), 148-167.

Fikar, C. R. (1992). The gay pediatrician: A report. *Journal of Homosexuality, 23*(3), 53-63.

Friskopp, A., & Silverstein, S. (1995). *Straight jobs, gay lives: Gay and lesbian professionals, the Harvard Business School, and the American workplace.* New York: Scribner.

Gonsiorek, J. (1993). Threat, stress, and adjustment: Mental health and the workplace for gay and lesbian individuals. In L. Diamant (Ed.), *Homosexual issues in the workplace* (pp. 243-264). Washington, DC: Taylor & Francis.

Griffin, C., & Zuckas, M. (1993). Coming out in psychology: Lesbian psychologists talk. *Feminism & Psychology, 3*(1), 111-133.

Hall, M. (1986). The lesbian corporate experience. *Journal of Homosexuality, 12*(3/4), 59-75.

Hetherington, C., Hillerbrand, E., & Etringer, B. (1989). Career counseling with gay men: Issues and recommendations. *Journal of Counseling and Development, 67,* 452-454.

Hetherington, C., & Orzek, A. (1989). Career counseling and life planning with lesbian women. *Journal of Counseling and Career Development, 68,* 52-57.

Kitzinger, C. (1991). Lesbians and gay men in the workplace: Psychological issues. In M. J. Davidson & J. Earnshaw (Eds.), *Vulnerable workers: Psychosocial and legal issues* (pp. 223-257). New York: John Wiley & Sons.

McNaught, B. (1993). *Gay issues in the workplace.* New York: St. Martin's Press.

McSpadden, J. R. (1993). Homosexuality and the church. In L. Diamant (Ed.), *Homosexual issues in the workplace* (pp. 91-103). Washington, DC: Taylor & Francis.

Melton, G. B. (1989). Public policy and private prejudice: Psychology and law on gay rights. *American Psychologist, 44*(6), 933-940.

Miller, G. V. (1995). *The gay male's odyssey in the corporate world: From disempowerment to empowerment.* New York: Harrington Park Press.

Morgan, K. S., & Brown, L. S. (1991). Lesbian career development, work behavior, and vocational counseling. *The Counseling Psychologist, 19*(2), 273-291.

National Association of Social Workers (1996). *Lesbian, gay and bisexual issues.* Washington, DC: Author.

Parker, S. G. (1994). Curing homophobia: Medicine begins to confront one of its last accepted prejudices. *New Physician, 43*(3), 12-19.

Pope, M. (1996). Gay and lesbian career counseling: Special career counseling issues. *Journal of Gay & Lesbian Social Services, 4*(4), 91-105.

Poverny, L. M., & Finch, W. A. (1988). Integrating work-related issues on gay and lesbian employees into occupational social work practice. *Employee Assistance Quarterly, 4*(2), 15-29.

Powers, B. (1996). The impact of gay, lesbian, and bisexual workplace issues on productivity. *Journal of Gay & Lesbian Social Services, 4*(4), 79-90.

Prince, J. P. (1995). Influences on the career development of gay men. *Career Development Quarterly, 44*(2), 168-77.

Rosabal, G. S. (1996). Multicultural existence in the workplace: Including how I thrive as a Latina lesbian feminist. *Journal of Gay & Lesbian Social Services, 4*(4), 17-28.

Roth, N. L., & Carman, J. (1993). Risk perception and HIV legal issues in the workplace. In L. Diamant (Ed.), *Homosexual issues in the workplace* (pp. 173-186). Washington, DC: Taylor & Francis.

Schneider, B. E. (1987). Coming out at work: Bridging the private/public gap. *Work and Occupations, 13*(4), 463-487.

Schneider, B. E. (1982). Consciousness about sexual harassment among heterosexual and lesbian women workers. *Journal of Social Issues, 38*(4), 75-98.

Seck, E. T., Finch, W. A., Mor-Barak, M. E., & Poverny, L. M. (1993). Managing a diverse workforce. *Administration in Social Work, 17*(2), 67-79.

Spielman, S., & Winfeld, L. (1996). Domestic partner benefits: A bottom line discussion. *Journal of Gay & Lesbian Social Services, 4*(4), 53-78.

Taylor, V., & Raeburn, N. C. (1995). Identity politics as high-risk activism: Career consequences for lesbian, gay, and bisexual sociologists. *Social Problems, 42*(2), 252-273.

Terry, P. (1992). Entitlement not privilege: The right of employment and advancement. In N. J. Woodman (Ed.), *Lesbian and gay lifestyles: A guide for counseling and education* (pp. 133-143). New York: Irvington Publishers.

VanDenBergh, N. (1994). From invisibility to voice: Providing EAP assistance to lesbians in the workplace. *Employee Assistance Quarterly, 9*(3/4), 161-177.

Van Soest, D. (1996). The influence of competing ideologies about homosexuality on nondiscrimination policy: Implications for social work education. *Journal of Social Work Education, 32*(1), 53-64.

Woods, J. D. (1993). *The corporate closet: The professional lives of gay men in America*. New York: Free Press.

Zuckerman, A, J., & Simons, G. F. (1996). *Sexual orientation in the workplace*. Thousand Oaks, CA: Sage Publications.

Mujer, Latina, Lesbiana–
Notes on the Multidimensionality
of Economic and Sociopolitical Injustice

Dorie Gilbert Martinez

SUMMARY. This paper examines the impact of economic and so-ciopolitical injustice on Latina lesbians on four dimensions of in-justice and oppression: (1) vigilance about anti-gay violence and sexual harassment/victimization, (2) employment discrimination, (3) marginalization by the larger, White lesbian and gay community, and (4) heterosexism within traditional, Hispanic communities. The layered effects of injustices combine to increase psychoemotional vulnerability for this group of women. Multiple challenges experi-enced by Latina lesbians highlight the fact that challenges presented by economic and sociopolitical injustice will remain challenges for lesbians of color even after such challenges are overcome by White gay males and, to some extent, White lesbians. Implications for gay/ lesbian services and the gay rights movement are discussed. *[Article copies available for a fee from The Haworth Document Delivery Service: 1-800-342-9678. E-mail address: getinfo@haworthpressinc.com]*

As a result of the gay rights movement, increasing attention is being given to the issue of social injustice against lesbians and gay men. While

Dorie Gilbert Martinez, PhD, is Assistant Professor, The University of Texas at Austin, 1925 San Jacinto Boulevard, Austin, TX 78712 (e-mail: dgm@mail. utexas. edu).

[Haworth co-indexing entry note]: "Mujer, Latina, Lesbiana–Notes on the Multidimensionality of Economic and Sociopolitical Injustice." Martinez, Dorie Gilbert. Co-published simultaneously in *Jour-nal of Gay & Lesbian Social Services* (The Haworth Press, Inc.) Vol. 8, No. 3, 1998, pp. 99-112; and: *Violence and Social Injustice Against Lesbian, Gay and Bisexual People* (ed: Lacey M. Sloan, and Nora S. Gustavsson) The Haworth Press, Inc., 1998, pp. 99-112. Single or multiple copies of this article are available for a fee from The Haworth Document Delivery Service [1-800-342-9678, 9:00 a.m. - 5:00 p.m. (EST). E-mail address: getinfo@haworthpressinc.com].

most literature highlighting the plight of lesbians and gay men has sought to treat them as a whole, gender and ethnic differences can influence the nature and extent of social injustices for subgroups of this population. From the perspective of the U. S. majority group, Latina[1] lesbians experience multiple vulnerabilities to economic and sociopolitical injustice–as women, as ethnic minorities, and as lesbians. Evidence of this multiple vulnerability to societal stigmatization and oppression based on gender, ethnicity, and sexual orientation is found in research exploring the nature of anti-gay and lesbian attitudes. Two studies showed that individuals who hold negative attitudes towards homosexuals are more likely to have sexist attitudes and favor double standards between men and women (Henley & Pincus, 1978; Milham, San Miguel, & Kellogg, 1976). It has also been noted that individuals who hold negative attitudes towards homosexuals are more likely to hold negative attitudes towards other minorities (Henley & Pincus, 1978). This paper discusses four themes of economic and sociopolitical injustice for Latina lesbians: anti-gay violence and sexual harassment, employment discrimination, marginalization by the White lesbian and gay community, and heterosexism within traditional, Hispanic communities.

REVIEW OF THE LITERATURE

For Latina lesbians, the complex interaction of gender, race, and sexual orientation would likely compound the experiences of oppression and nonacceptance in a sexist, racist, and heterosexist society. For example, regardless of sexual orientation, gender discrepancies continue to exist, resulting in lower pay, unequal educational opportunities, and decreased economic and political power for women. Thus, because women in general are less likely to be employed in high-status positions, lesbians would be expected to endure more economic and social injustices than men, on average.

Within the larger group of lesbians in the U. S., lesbians of color[2] would be expected to have different sociopolitical experiences, based on societal and institutional discrimination against Hispanics, African Americans, and other ethnic minorities. Recent concern has been raised regarding the persistent polarization between ethnic minorities and Whites, reflected by survey findings that White people continue to avoid close, frequent, or prolonged contact with ethnic minority group members (Curran & Renzetti, 1993). Like African Americans, Hispanic Americans fare less well than Whites across many areas, including lower educational attainment, poorer housing, higher unemployment, and more job discrimination (National

Association of Hispanic Publications, 1995). Hispanic Americans' continued struggle for economic and sociopolitical power recently sparked the 1996 First Hispanic March on Washington, DC, highlighting these continued inequities. Moreover, conservative movements such as California's Propositions 187 and 209 and the English language-only proposals have increased the precarious state of Hispanics in this country.

Furthermore, the period of political and social conservatism witnessed during the 1980s has continued, and in some cases, increased throughout the 1990s, with implications for both lesbians and gay men and ethnic minorities. The conservative attitude of many directed against homosexuals, in general, is one of denouncing gay men and lesbians as immoral (Herek, 1994). Adam (1995, p. 144) notes that gay people are currently threatened by "neoconservative movements to restore privileges of patriarchy, white domination, and lost imperial grandeur–a vision from which gay people remain always excluded." Adam (1995) also notes that, indeed, it is a vision from which lesbians of color are even further excluded.

For lesbians of color, ethnic-based discrimination may exist not only from the larger society but also from within the majority White, mainstream gay and lesbian community. For instance, Loiacano (1989) noted that the lesbian community and lesbian social groups may not, as a whole, readily embrace lesbians of color. Furthermore, some argue that within traditional Hispanic communities, Latina lesbians face another level of oppression. Trujillo (1991) notes that Chicana lesbians must face obstacles within the culture based on religion, family, and loyalty to the race. As has been noted in the literature on African American gays, lesbians and gay men of color may receive harsher treatment and condemnation from their own community than that of the larger, White community (Earnst, Francis, Nevels, & Lemeh, 1991; Icard, 1986).

A number of Latina lesbian writers have expressed their views in an anthology of prose, poetry and essays in an effort to decrease the isolation experienced by many Latina lesbians (Ramos, 1994). Vazquez (1993, p. 217) describes the U. S. lesbian/gay movement as being divided between "those who view the struggle for lesbian and gay liberation through the single lens of oppression on the basis of sexual orientation and those who view it through a prism." Vazquez (1993) further adds that effective political coalition within the movement has been hampered in two ways:

> both by the single lens focus on oppression based on sexual orientation and the misguided notion that we can address racism and sexism within our own movement through consciousness raising without a

political agenda that specifically addresses racism, sexism, and economic injustice. . . . As a Latina and a lesbian, I cannot reduce what I understand about oppression and political repression in the United States to heterosexism. (p. 223)

Thus, the failure to fully consider the impact of the intersection of race/ethnicity, gender, and sexual orientation has the effect of rendering lesbians of color invisible. This invisibility is also reflected in the dearth of statistics and research on Latina lesbians. In one study, Hidalgo and Hidalgo-Christensen (1976-1977) examined the experiences of Puerto Rican lesbians and the response of the Puerto Rican community. In another study on lesbian identity development, Espin (1987) published the results of a brief survey of a small sample of Cuban lesbians. Both studies documented the need for further discussion about the unique experiences of Latina lesbians. Focusing primarily on Mexican American lesbians, this paper highlights major life challenges impacting Latina lesbians and draws attention to the need for further research on the concerns of these women.

THEMES OF ECONOMIC AND SOCIOPOLITICAL INJUSTICE

Multiple factors create economic and sociopolitical dynamics which combine to increase the vulnerability of Latina lesbians. The following discussion explores the realities faced by many Latina lesbians by examining four themes of economic and sociopolitical injustice: anti-gay violence and sexual harassment, employment discrimination, marginalization by the broader gay and lesbian group, and oftentimes, fear of rejection from a traditional family and community. Based on excerpts from a focus group interview with a group of Latina lesbians (Martinez & Casanova, 1997),[3] relevant literature, and practice knowledge, the author addresses how and to what extent Latina lesbians may be more challenged by sociopolitical and economic injustices beyond what the larger community of White lesbian and gay men experience. The discussion is meant to increase awareness of the unique challenges which exist when considering the intersection of race/ethnicity, gender, and sexual orientation for Latina lesbians.

Vigilance About Gay Bashing, Violence, and Sexual Harassment

Although more gay men than lesbians are victims of anti-gay/lesbian violence (Comstock, 1991), non-victimized lesbians may experience a vicarious trauma related to their knowledge of frequent violence against their male counterparts. They frequently develop a keen awareness or vigilance about their own vulnerability to gay bashing. More importantly, among lesbians who are victims of anti-gay violence, Comstock (1991) found that a greater proportion of lesbians of color seem to experience violence. Moreover, among the various social classes, women from lower class backgrounds were more frequent victims than women from middle or upper class backgrounds (Comstock, 1991). Although Comstock reports these as tentative conclusions, the findings point, again, to the potential multidimensionality of injustice experienced by Latina lesbians, particularly lower class Latina lesbians.

In addition to class, the vicissitudes resulting from both racism and homophobia increase the risk of victimization and sociopolitical injustice for all gays of color. Jessie, who had been out 11 years, described the lack of response to the murders of several Latino gay males in a small, Latino community:

> These men were picked up from a popular cruising park, taken out to the fields, and brutally murdered and dismembered, and the police basically ignored it. I think they look at it like we're just trash anyway, like we're expendable.

In addition to the vulnerability faced in the larger society, vigilance about anti-gay violence is also a great concern for Latina lesbians when interacting with a community which has a strongly-entrenched, traditional Latino culture. One woman pointed out, "If you go somewhere in the Latino community, and you want to be affectionate with your girlfriend, you feel people staring at you, and it's scary." Because Latina lesbians will most likely interact with three communities–the general public, the gay community, and the Latino community–the vigilance becomes tied to the coming out process. In essence, for these women, coming out is a daily process as they are forced to constantly make decisions about which situations are safe within the various communities which they enter and exit daily.

One oft-neglected topic is sexual harassment and violence directed at lesbian women by heterosexual men. Like their heterosexual counterparts, lesbians face a constant threat of physical and sexual violence in our society, simply based on their gender. However, lesbians are usually aware of the unique threat posed by straight men who attempt to prey on lesbian women and experience a heightened concern about potential sexual harassment and victimization, particularly regarding straight men who visit lesbian and mixed (gay men and lesbian) bars. The following comment addresses the concern about this issue.

> Heterosexual men don't tend to take heterosexual women's relationships seriously, much less that of lesbians. It's like they're convinced we really want a sexual encounter with them.

Of interest is Comstock's (1991) findings that regardless of gender, between 3 percent and 16 percent of gays and lesbians reported being raped because of their sexual orientation; for women the range was between 4 percent and 18 percent. Duncan (1990) reported that forced sex experiences among lesbian women were higher than those of heterosexual college women. Compounding this issue for Latina lesbians is the stereotype of the "sexually-deprived lesbian" and the sexual myth of the "hot, Latin woman" which increase their risk of sexual harassment and victimization.

In summing up the result of this double-jeopardy stereotype, Hammonds (1995, p. 410) aptly points out that people of color still contend with the myth that "certain 'groups' of people [do not] have the same ability to exercise control over their sexual behavior and drives as 'normal' white heterosexuals do." As long as such views are prevalent in the dominant society, lesbians of color will suffer disproportionate, negative effects.

Multiple Discrimination in Employment

The combination of sexism, racism, and heterosexism in employment practices is a serious concern for Latina lesbians in that they may experience discrimination in the workplace on several levels. In describing her experience with the U. S. military, Mary, a lesbian for 5 years, described the former ban against gays and the more recent "don't ask, don't tell" policy as oppressive, cutting at her very existence. For young adults who have relatively few educational and career opportunities, joining the military may be one of the few career opportunities, reflected in the relatively large number of Hispanics and African Americans in the military. Thus, the dilemma of being oneself versus being kept down economically was difficult to negotiate. For example, Mary explained her experience in this way:

> For me, my goals, education, benefits, and future depended on making sure that I never acted in any way that gave any one the least suspicion. My future depended on it. Yet, my life was filled with hiding and fear.

Having worked for a large, corporate office, another woman described her experience of anti-gay/lesbian discrimination:

> When I started, they said we could put up anything we wanted in our personal cubicles. Well, I put up a small flyer about a lesbian re-source center. They asked me to take it down, even though it was consistent with types of items allowed according to the policy and procedures manual. . . . And this was a company that stipulated in their hiring practices no discrimination based on race, sex, and sexual orientation, etc.

Instances of discrimination based on their ethnicity may result in deep pain as many Latina lesbians are reminded of the historical economic and political oppression of their Mexican American ancestors. In addition, dealing with racial/ethnic prejudice in the workplace can result in stress and feelings of powerlessness. In referring to ethnic bias within the workplace, Sylvia stated, "The thing about discrimination now is that it's really subtle. You just deal with it, you don't even think about it. Some of it you just expect and you just deal with it." However, Mary disagreed, making the case that much of the discrimination is still overt. She then recounted an interview experience in which she was told, first subtly and then bla-tantly, by the interviewer that she was not "top caliber," referring to her ethnicity.

Since discrimination in the employment arena has implications for one's overall psychological well-being and adjustment (Cass, 1979; Cain, 1990), Latina lesbians will most likely be psychologically challenged by their employment related stress given their multiple vulnerabilities. Ellis and Riggle (1995) found a positive relationship between working in envi-ronments with policies prohibiting discrimination on the basis of sexual orientation and overall job satisfaction. Thus, having to hide one's identity within an anti-gay/lesbian work environment likely leads to lowered life satisfaction if other supports are not available to women. Given that sup-port for the hypothesis that job satisfaction "spills over" to life satisfac-tion has been documented (Rain, Lane, & Sterner, 1991), it can be said that Latina lesbians may suffer from negative, psychoemotional effects when job/career options are limited due to one or more social oppressions.

A Sense of Marginalization from the Larger Gay and Lesbian Community

Lesbians are at times subjected to the sexism that is practiced by some gay men, evident by the fact that lesbians are sometimes barred from certain gay male-dominated social establishments. However, subtle and overt discrimination aimed to keep both women and/or people of color off limits to male and/or White male, gay bars is also common, meaning that lesbians of color are marginalized to various degrees from the mainstream gay and lesbian community. The sense of marginalization for these women is based first on their ethnicity and compounded by sexism and classism. A poignant comment from a focus group participant illustrates this point.

> . . . Whether you are a woman, whether you're a woman of color, whether you're a lesbian, whether you're working class, if you're an immigrant, I mean, you can push people out to the edge. The gay and lesbian white community can be very mainstream, to adopt mainstream ideas, which to me seem to also be discriminatory, especially economically.

Based on ethnic differences within the general society, economic disparities will exist between gays and lesbians of color and their White gay and lesbian counterparts. In comparison to their White lesbian counterparts, Latina lesbians will likely have more difficult life challenges and, in turn, their struggles within the gay and lesbian rights movement are multiple and complex. A salient issue in the sense of maginalization felt by Latina lesbians is the fact that homophobia is the only barrier to White, gay male privilege. Moreover, Molina (1994) contends that often White lesbians see themselves as having only one identity: lesbian. On the other hand, Latina lesbians have ethnicity as a strong reference point and are constantly aware of the potential racism emanating from both the larger society and the broader gay and lesbian community. As Hemphill (1991) points out, acknowledging their gay identity does not necessarily mean that White gays and lesbians transcend their racist conditioning. Thus, for Latina lesbians and other lesbians of color, attending functions where they may be in the minority may raise issues of potential discrimination, covert or overt, from their White counterparts.

In a qualitative study with a small sample of Black lesbians, researchers found that perceived prejudice impacts not only their involvement in mainstream lesbian activities but also their intimate relationships with White lesbians (Mays, Cochran, & Rhue, 1993). As is the case with other lesbians of color, interracial partner selection can take on a unique meaning. One Latina lesbian expressed this sentiment, "This whole idea that somehow White is better and I see Latina women chasing after the few white women that are there. It's so painful to watch." For some, this is more than the taboo associated with interracial relationships, but rather what has been referred to as "colonizer/colonized relationships" (de Alba,

1993, p. 960), with controversial implications within the Latina lesbian community.

Among the many reasons for choosing a White partner, a Latina lesbian may be experiencing internalized racism or may be seeking to increase her power and perceived status in society. However, as experienced by one African American lesbian interviewee in the Mays et al. (1993) study, an interracial relationship may then increase the level of discrimination against the interracial couple in housing, employment, and in the general public.

Nonacceptance by Traditional Hispanic Community

To the extent that their families are traditional Hispanic families, Latina lesbians may be less accepted by their families and cultural communities than their White lesbian counterparts. In discussing the atmosphere of living as a Latina lesbian in a traditional, Hispanic community, this was one reaction: "You don't. To be out–gay or lesbian–well, you just don't, we're talking life-threatening." To some Latina lesbians, the fear of coming out to their families is intense. However, because overt acknowledgment of lesbianism is relatively more restricted in the traditional, Hispanic culture than in mainstream American society (Espin, 1995; Hidalgo & Hidalgo-Christensen, 1976-77), many Latina lesbians are faced with the stress of managing two identities. For some, this may mean being accepted with a "silent tolerance" or unspoken acknowledgment by their immediate families (Espin, 1987).

Traditional gender-roles are often expected of females in a traditional, Hispanic setting. Patriarchal attitudes that exist in traditional Hispanic communities result in deeply-entrenched sex role standards and less acceptance of strong, independent females by male Hispanics. A focus group participant felt that "lesbians are not accepted because after dealing with all these issues we emerge as strong women, which, in turn, is not easily accepted by the male." The sense of a shared experience with societal discrimination and exposure to traditional, machismo increased this participant's sense of solidarity with Latina, heterosexual women. Comments from the interview excerpts were consistent with writings by Trujillo (1991, p. 191) that:

> Chicana lesbians pose a threat to the Chicano community primarily because they threaten the established social hierarchy of patriarchal control. In her failure to take on one of the accepted roles–mother, wife, virgin, or whore–she neither propagates the race nor meets the needs of the macho male.

For Latina albinos, the extent to which religion, mainly Catholicism, and traditional Hispanic culture characterizes the family of origin and/or extended family greatly impacts their relationship with their families and the degree to which they are "out" to their families. In her survey of 16 Cuban lesbians, Espin (1987, p. 47) found that:

> When confronted with the choice of being among Latins without coming out, or living among lesbians who are not Latin or who are unfamiliar with Latin culture, 11 [of 16] women said they had chosen or would choose the second alternative.

Nevertheless, this choice is often made with much ambivalence, anger, and pain. Of great concern is the deep sense of isolation the women may experience as a result of marginalization from the mainstream White lesbian and gay community which, in turn, forces them to rely more on their nonaccepting families and the Hispanic community for support. In cases where there is no family support and the woman is simultaneously shut out by the Hispanic community, the sense of oppressive isolation is confounded. Labeled as a "vendida," or sellout (Trujillo, 1991, p. 191) or described as a "Malinchista" (traitor) to the race (de Alba, 1993, p. 962), the Latina lesbian then becomes marginalized from both within the Latino culture and from the outer mainstream society, including mainstream lesbian and gay communities.

On the other hand, some Latina lesbians are "out" to both their families and the gay/lesbian community. In such cases, a strong family cohesiveness can provide crucial support in dealing with the societal injustices. For instance, a Latina lesbian noted that when visiting her parents, who live in a traditional Hispanic bordertown, the family becomes more supportive of her because they themselves are aware of the danger she faces from that Hispanic community, in terms of potential gay/lesbian bashing and hate crimes.

CONCLUSION AND PRACTICE IMPLICATIONS

This paper explored common themes and variables related to the multiple vulnerability experienced by Latina lesbians. There is no monolithic group of Latina lesbians; however, the insights offered here are of importance for future research efforts as well as social services. In sum, the experiences of many Latina lesbians tend to highlight and support much of the existing knowledge regarding anti-gay/lesbian violence and discriminatory practices based on gender, ethnicity, and sexual orientation. Special attention was drawn to the intersection of gender and ethnicity which creates unique challenges for Latina lesbians within both the larger, White lesbian and gay male community as well as within traditional Hispanic communities.

Given the precarious state of lesbians of color both within the general public and within the Hispanic community, they are at increased risk for violence based on sexual orientation. Additionally, they may be targeted more by perpetrators in the general public due to both their ethnicity and their sexual orientation. Of particular concern is the women's experiences with heterosexual sexual harassment. More research and exploration in this area is needed to ensure that rape prevention and anti-sexual assault programs are meeting the needs of lesbians and providing culturally-sensitive services for lesbians of color.

Latina lesbians may encounter occupational discrimination based on all three variables–gender, ethnicity, and sexual orientation. This may place them at greater risk for unemployment, lower pay, and limited career options. The women may experience increased psychological burdens related to job discrimination and economic inequities. In addition, Latina lesbians and gays of color may experience a strong sense of being marginalized from the White, mainstream lesbian and gay community; however, the extent to which Latina lesbians experience individual, psychological trauma related to this issue requires an in-depth study. In addition, more research should explore the impact of perceived prejudice on interracial friendships and mate selection among lesbians.

Finally, Latina lesbians often contend with oppression from within the Hispanic community and their lack of acceptance by those with whom they share common ethnic-based injustices. Because family and community are important variables in most Hispanics cultures, Latina lesbians may suffer from increased psychoemotional vulnerability. Having a safe space available where Latina lesbians can meet similar others seems crucial to their well-being. However, the women may not readily seek out psychotherapy. One woman discussed how she was taught not to seek out help for psychological or emotional needs and recounted how the topic was "taboo" and her own processes of recognizing the need to ask for help. Because other Latina lesbians may have had the same teachings, more rap or discussion groups are recommended to bring Latina lesbians together to discuss their common issues and enhance support systems. Practitioners should be aware that their role in helping Latina lesbians is multifaceted, involving both individual and societal dimensions.

The overall implications for the gay rights movement are complex. The concerns mentioned here exist around economic and sociopolitical injustice, challenges that when overcome by White gay males and, to some extent, White lesbians, will remain challenges for lesbians of color. An active, open dialogue is needed within the gay rights movement about the extent to which White, gay men, but more so, White lesbians, as a whole, can comprehend the broader issues of oppression for lesbians of color. Finally, the very concerns raised here highlight the continued debate regarding whether the feminist and lesbian feminist paradigms fully embrace the goal of ending all oppression.

Further research and more comprehensive knowledge about the issues discussed here are needed. However, by noting the concerns raised here, social service providers can begin to consider ways in which social action and services can more effectively serve the needs of Latina lesbians.

NOTES

1. The terms Latina/o, Chicana/o, Hispanic, and Mexican American are used interchangeably throughout the text. However, an individual's preference for a particular term is based on regional, age, cultural, and philosophical differences.

2. The term lesbian of color in this article will be used to refer to all groups of lesbians included in the term Hispanic, as well as African American and other ethnic minority groups of lesbians who share the experience of being historically and/or currently oppressed in the U. S. society.

3. A small group of Mexican-American lesbians participated in a focus group discussion on social injustice. The women were all young, Mexican-American lesbians who were part of an openly gay, Latina lesbian organization. None of the women were out to their family members, who, for all of the women, lived in a different city. Names, when used, have been changed to conceal identities.

REFERENCES

Adam, B. D. (1995). *The rise of a gay and lesbian movement.* New York: Twayne.
Cain, R. (1990). Homosexual identity and gay identity development. *Social Work, 36,* 67-73.
Cass, V. (1979). Homosexual identity formation: A theoretical model. *Journal of Homosexuality, 4,* 219-235.
Comstock, G. D. (1991). *Violence against lesbians and gay men.* New York: Columbia University Press.
Curran, D. J., & Renzetti, C. M. (1993). *Social problems.* Boston, MA: Allyn and Bacon.
de Alba, A. G. (1993). Tortillerismo: Work by Chicana lesbians. *Signs: Journal of Women in Culture and Society, 18*(4), 956-963.

Duncan, D. F. (1990). Prevalence of sexual assault victimization among hetero-sexual and gay/lesbian university students. *Psychological Reports, 66*, 65-66.

Earnst, F. A., Francis, R. A., Nevels, H., & Lemeh, C. A. (1991). Condemnation of homosexuality in the Black community: A gender-specific phenomenon? *Archives of Sexual Behavior, 20*(6), 579-585.

Ellis, A. L., & Riggle, E. D. (1995). The relation of job satisfaction and degree of openness about one's sexual orientation for lesbians and gay men. *Journal of Homosexuality, 30*(2), 75-85.

Espin, O. M. (1987). Issues in identity in the psychology of Latina lesbians. In Boston Lesbian Psychologies Collective (Ed.), *Lesbian psychologies: Explorations and challenges.* (pp. 35-51). Chicago, IL: University of Illinois Press.

Espin, O. M. (1995). Cultural and historical influences on sexuality in Hispanic/Latin women: Implications for psychotherapy. In M. L. Andersen & P. H. Collins (Eds.), *Race, class, and gender: An anthology* (pp. 423-428). Belmont, CA: Wadsworth Publishing Company.

Hammonds, E. (1995). Race, sex, and AIDS: The construction of "other." In M. L. Andersen & P. H. Collins (Eds.), *Race, class, and gender: An anthology* (pp. 402-413). Belmont, CA: Wadsworth Publishing Company.

Hemphill, E. (Ed.). (1991). *Brother to brother: New writings by Black gay men.* Boston: Alyson Publications.

Henley, N. M., & Pincus, F. (1978). Interrelationships of sexist, racist, and anti-homosexual attitudes. *Psychological Reports, 42*, 83-90.

Herek, G. M. (1994). Assessing attitudes toward lesbians and gay men: A review of empirical research with the ATLG scale. In B. Greene & G. M. Herek (Eds.), *Lesbian and gay psychology: Theory, research, and clinical applications* (pp. 206-228). Thousand Oaks, CA: Sage.

Hidalgo, H., & Hidalgo-Christensen, E. (1976-77). The Puerto Rican lesbian and the Puerto Rican community. *Journal of Homosexuality, 2*, 109-21.

Icard, L. (1986). Black gay men and conflicting social identities: Sexual orientation versus racial identity. *Journal of Social Work and Human Sexuality, 4*, 83-93.

Loiacano, D. K. (1989). Gay identity issues among Black Americans: Racism, homophobia, and the need for validation. *Journal of Counseling and Development, 68*, 21-25.

Martinez, D. G., & Casanova, M. C. (1997, May). *Latina lesbians: Conflict between culture and society.* Paper presented at the Texas Lesbian Conference, Houston, TX.

Mays, V. M., Cochran, S. D., & Rhue, S. (1993). The impact of perceived discrimination on the intimate relationships of Black lesbians. *Journal of Homosexuality, 25*(4), 1-14.

Millham, J., San Miguel, C. L., & Kellogg, R. (1976). A factor-analytic conceptualization of attitudes toward male and female homosexuals. *Journal of Homosexuality, 2*, 3-10.

Molina, M. L. (1994). Fragmentations: Meditations on separatism. *Signs: Journal of Women in Culture and Society, 19*(2), 449-457.

National Association of Hispanic Publications (1995). *Hispanics-Latinos: Diverse people in a multicultural society. A special report.* Washington, DC.

Rain, J. S., Lane, I. M., & Steiner, D. D. (1991). A current look at the job satisfaction/life satisfaction relationships: Review for future considerations. *Human Relations, 44,* 287-307.

Ramos, J. (Ed.). (1994). *Companeros: Latina lesbians.* New York: Routledge.

Trujillo, C. (1991). *Chicana lesbians: The girls our mothers warned us about.* Merkeley: Third Woman.

Vazquez, C. (1993). The land that never has been yet: Dreams of a gay Latina in the United States. In A. Hendriks, R. Tielman, & E. van der Veen (Eds.), *The third pink book: A global view of lesbian and gay liberation and oppression* (pp. 217-225). Buffalo, NY: International Lesbian and Gay Association.

Homosexuality and Latinos/as: Towards an Integration of Identities

Flavio Francisco Marsiglia

SUMMARY. This paper explores the relationship between ethnic, gender, and sexual identities among Latinos/as from a developmental perspective. Culturally prescribed gender roles are explored and lack of support from the indigenous communities are discussed as oppressive factors that inhibit a healthier integration of both ethnic and sexual identities. The role social workers can play in facilitating the integration of these identities and other recommendations are provided within a culturally grounded approach. *[Article copies available for a fee from The Haworth Document Delivery Service: 1-800-342-9678. E-mail address: getinfo@haworthpressinc.com]*

Lesbian and gay Latinas and Latinos face multiple challenges in trying to integrate their sexual, gender, and ethnic identities. This article examines some of these issues, outlines sources of conflict and oppression, and highlights strategies social workers can use in confronting oppression and supporting sexual diversity.

Understanding and celebrating sexuality is an ongoing journey that cannot be taken in isolation from other dimensions of the human experience. As part of this process, we look at ourselves through the lenses of culture and personal stories. The narratives or explanations of who we are

Flavio Francisco Marsiglia, PhD, is Assistant Professor, School of Social Work, Arizona State University, Box 871802, Tempe, AZ 85287-1802 (e-mail: fla99@imap1.asu.edu).

[Haworth co-indexing entry note]: "Homosexuality and Latinos/as: Towards an Integration of Identities." Marsiglia, Flavio Francisco. Co-published simultaneously in *Journal of Gay & Lesbian Social Services* (The Haworth Press, Inc.) Vol. 8, No. 3, 1998, pp. 113-125; and: *Violence and Social Injustice Against Lesbian, Gay and Bisexual People* (ed: Lacey M. Sloan, and Nora S. Gustavsson) The Haworth Press, Inc., 1998, pp. 113-125. Single or multiple copies of this article are available for a fee from The Haworth Document Delivery Service [1-800-342-9678, 9:00 a.m. - 5:00 p.m. (EST). E-mail address: getinfo@haworthpressinc.com].

113

may not conform to conventional labels or definitions. As Frank Browning (1996, p. 7) suggests "we cannot tell our sexual story, 'gay' or 'straight,' free of other stories of grief, loss, love, expectations, and dreams . . . ." He further advises the reader to be open and generous towards sexual geographies that are organized in ways other than their own. The Latino experience with sexuality is an example of a unique geography. Latinos and Latinas as a people have a long and proud history in the United States and during that time they have accumulated their share of grief and dreams. Their sexual "geographies" cannot be explored disconnected from their ethnic identities, their histories of oppression, and their overall narrative as a people. The Latino gay, lesbian and bisexual experience can be characterized as the experience of a pan-ethnic (Espiritu, 1992; Oboler, 1995) and polyvalent community (Geschwender, 1992). Social experiences of Latinos and Latinas cannot be reduced to a single experience. Exploring Latino sexual geographies implies a dynamic and fluid journey through the rich Latino cultural continuum and its interaction with majority society (i.e., cultural preservation and the acculturation process).

INTERACTING WITH THE GAY COMMUNITY

Some Latinas and Latinos experiencing same-gender affectionate-erotic feelings and practices may not self-identify with the mainstream gay community. The gay community implies in part the embracing of a collective action agenda and the development of certain criteria of who is and who is not part of the community. Gay and lesbian activists express concern about the lack of involvement of Latinos and Latinas in the mainstream gay community. Definitions about sexual orientation are often drawn from one cultural view point and viable choices are not provided to those who may perceive themselves as being different from majority society. The history of exclusion and oppression experienced by many Latino communities in the United States can be reproduced within the gay community. The pressure Latinos feel to conform to the majority culture is not just a heterosexual phenomenon. Latinas and Latinos self-identifying as lesbian or gay may confront an apparent group allegiance dilemma: Are we Latinas and Latinos or are we lesbian or gay? Sexual identity and ethnic identity are often seen as mutually exclusive. Latinos/as may feel pressure to abandon their ethnic identities in order to embrace their gay, lesbian, bisexual, or transgender identities.

Latina lesbian and Latino gay male identity development appear to require individuals to reconcile and integrate the culture of their family and community of origin with the gay community's culture. Some Latinos perceive gay and lesbian culture as a white middle class phenomenon that is alien to their own ethnic group. The gay and lesbian community has developed a unique and effective symbolic array of practices and rituals that define and reinforce boundaries between the gay-minority culture and the heterosexual-dominant culture. These practices and "codes" may not be part of the experiential repertoire of Latinos having same-gender affectionate-erotic feelings and practices. If Latinas and Latinos have to leave the fold of their families and communities of origin to become whole sexually, they in turn may run the risk of becoming culturally deprived and oppressed. However, abandoning their communities and families of origin appears to be the only alternative available for some Latinos and Latinas who want to openly express their sexuality. Latino community members often perceive lesbians and gay men as challenging or violating social expectations. This is due to their personal lifestyles and because they are placing personal desires above the needs of their family or the community (Almaro, 1978; Kanuha, 1990).

This double oppression of not being represented in the gay and lesbian mainstream culture and not being accepted as gay or lesbian in their ethnic communities may limit individual Latina lesbians and Latino gay men in their ability to integrate their sexual and ethnic identities. Social workers can play an important role as cultural mediators in assisting individuals to integrate their multiple identities. In order to serve in this role, social workers need to become familiar with the community history and cultural legacy of their clients. In order to affirm ethnic and sexual identity, the professional needs to become familiar with the indigenous narratives developed by the client and her or his community. It is also prudent to explore the interacting effects of social class, ethnicity, gender, and sexual orientation. These interactions will generate a unique cosmology and language. Language is far more complex than English or Spanish. Language becomes the repository of possibilities or perceived barriers towards a celebration and integration of sexual and ethnic identities. Perhaps there is a need to create a more inclusive language that will allow for more inclusive narratives. Social workers imposing an ethnocentric gay and lesbian language may be doing a disservice to the Latino or Latina client in need of help. Culture and language are intimately connected and they need to be understood as one.

LATINOS AND LATINAS IN CONTEXT

Traditional Latinos and Latinas see family and ethnic community as the primary reference group (Organista, 1996). Cooperation, interdependence and strong commitment to the extended family are paramount. Kinship, both consanguine and affinal, is the primary bond and prescribes the strongest rights and duties. The Latino community with its own set of beliefs and practices can impede a healthy integration of Latino gays and Latina lesbians' sexual and ethnic identities. On the other hand, the mainstream gay community has its share of discrimination against and ignorance about the Latino community. Gender or sexual stereotypes are commonly linked with ethnic and racial stereotypes (Icard, 1985, 1986; Woodman, Kawasaki, & Mayeda, 1983). Within the gay men and lesbian communities, ethnic and racial discrimination can lead to ignoring, rejecting, or perceiving minority individuals as exotic (Chan, 1989). Lesbian and gay Latino people may feel like outcasts within their own ethnic communities and misunderstood or discriminated against within the mainstream lesbian and gay community. They may be oppressed by their community of origin and its strict cultural norms and at the same time they can be oppressed by a gay culture that does not recognize their unique culture and world view. Latina lesbians, Latino gay men and bisexuals often live three different lives among three distinct communities: the gay and lesbian community, the Latino community, and the predominantly heterosexual non-Latino White mainstream community (Morales, 1990). Latina lesbians, Latino gays and bisexuals may experience a triple stigma and oppression when they are not fully accepted in the gay community because of their ethnicity, rejected by their community of origin because of their sexual orientation, and discriminated against by the majority culture because of their ethnicity and sexual orientation (Yep, 1995). This paper explores alternatives to these potentially oppressive situations through a more generous integration of identities.

THE DEVELOPMENTAL APPROACH

The developmental approach can guide us in the construction of a more liberating relationship between ethnic and sexual identities among gay and lesbian Latinos/as. The developmental approach studies the relationship between culture and human development. The main exponent of this school of thought is the Byelorussian psychologist Lev Vygostky (1979). He maintained that humans are active, vigorous participants in their existence. At each stage of development they acquire the means by which they can completely affect their world and themselves. Vygostky identifies auxiliary stimuli as components of a process experienced by humans for active adaptation. Auxiliary stimuli may include the tools of the culture in which the child was born. Stimuli are practices, beliefs, and traditions.

Paulo Freire's (1995) constructs on Liberation Pedagogy are based in part in Vygostky's research. Freire expands on the developmental framework and explores the idea of oppression and liberation from oppression as collective constructs based on a collective definition of the environment. In the course of human development, according to this approach, psychological systems arise which unite separate functions into new combinations and complexes. Historical conditions, which to a large extent determine the opportunities for human experience, are constantly changing. Thus, there cannot be a universal scheme that adequately represents the dynamic relationship between the external and the internal aspects of development.

From a developmental perspective, it is not possible to speak about a "culture or ethnic free" lesbian or gay male identity. Instead, sexual identity needs to be viewed as influenced by a complex interaction of biology, culture, history, and psychological influences (Garnets & Kimmel, 1991). Ethnicity needs to be treated as a source of energy and connectedness and as Foucault (1990) stated, homosexuality needs to be seen as a rich source of creative resistance. This integration of identities will be particularly relevant for Latinos and Latinas.

Although Spanish was the first Indo-European language spoken in what is today the United States, Spanish speaking people have had a long history of oppression and discrimination in this country. Latinos have been defined as an internally colonized people (Blauner, 1976). Anglos (i.e., English speakers) migrated illegally into Texas, which was then part of Mexico, in greater and greater numbers and gradually drove the *tejanos* from their lands, committing atrocities against them (Anzaldua, 1987). In addition, the Amerindian, Mestizo, and African roots of most Latinos/as make them phenotypically "different" from the Euroamerican majority. The colonization experience and their darker skin pigmentation makes Latino acculturation and assimilation experiences different from those experienced by European immigrants coming from non-English speaking countries. As a result, Latino culture is often perceived and misrepresented as exotic or primitive, and in need of redemption (Marsiglia & Zorita, 1996).

Heterogeneity is one of the most distinctive characteristics of the Latino communities in the United States. Felix Padilla (1985) defines the Latino ethnic identity as a situational operative identity and not based on one genuine national/cultural heritage passed down through generations. Latinos are a multiracial and multicultural group. Latino cultural symbols are fluid and not fixed in space or time. There are, however, some cultural descriptors that are commonly used in the literature to characterize the Latino cultures. They emerge as a synthesis of the Latino community's

Latin American character and its American influences. These aspects which transcend class lines are: language, the importance of the extended family, ritual kinship, male dominance, and the double sex standard (Rueschenberg & Buriel, 1995). In addition, gender roles are significant in both heterosexual and homosexual relationships.

GENDER ROLES

Gender roles tend to be polarized among Latino people and produce harsh role expectations. The male role is often called *Machismo* and the female role is described as *Marianismo*. Machismo is a socially constructed, learned, and reinforced set of behaviors comprising the content of male gender roles in Latino society (De la Cancela, 1981, 1986). Machismo is sometimes narrowly linked with sexual potency, or physical courage, but in reality it extends beyond that. It includes the belief that men are innately superior to women, and it affects the whole pattern of family relationships (Marin, 1989). Machismo suggests a protective attitude toward women, which also encourages promiscuity. The macho is the ideal personality for which men strive.

The macho is the man who is confident of his inner worth. He expresses his confidence in action or, if he is a politician or an intellectual, in words. The complete macho may become a caudillo (charismatic, non-democratic leader) because he personifies the aspirations of other men. Zaretsky (1976) speaks about machismo as an ideology that alienates men from themselves and their families. Machismo has been institutionalized through the division of labor between the work done in the home and that done for a salary under the agricultural and industrial systems. However, in the United States the term machismo has a clear racist connotation and serves to rank men according to their presumably national and racial characters. Machismo has been associated with negative character traits not among men in general but specifically among Mexican, Mexican American, and other Latino men (Gutmann, 1996). Machismo can be attributed to the socioeconomic status of Latino males (Davis & Chavez, 1995). As the division of labor between women and men changes and Latino males become active members of the household team, the negative connotations attached to traditional machismo will dissipate.

Marianismo is the traditional and culturally prescribed role of women. Marianismo derives from María, mother of God and virgin in the Catholic tradition. The concept underlying "Marianismo" is that women are spiritually superior to men, and therefore can endure all suffering inflicted by men (Stevens, 1973). The "marianista" code rewards women who adhere to it. Due to the sacredness ascribed to motherhood in traditional Latino cultures, women who bear children enjoy a certain degree of power despite the apparent outward submissiveness of their behavior. As women grow older, they attain a semi-divine status, in which adult offspring ally with their mothers' struggles, especially against their fathers. Therefore, power is achieved by women through passivity and by conforming to the "marianista" role (Comas-Diaz, 1987).

Due to the importance ascribed to marriage and motherhood, women are brought up to be responsible and to seek a man who is serious. A traditional young woman rarely has more than one or two "novios" (steady boyfriends) before marrying, while a young man may have an unlimited number of "novias." In traditional families, if a young couple date each other several times, it is assumed that the "noviazgo" (formal courtship) and "la boda" (the wedding) will inevitably follow. The Spanish words "novio" and "novia" can mean both bride and groom, or girlfriend and boyfriend. This illustrates the short bridge between dating and marriage (Wagenheim, 1970).

These polarized heterosexual norms tend to be transferred to same gender relationships. The value assigned to procreation, marriage, and "la familia" can be present in Latino gay and lesbian relationships through commitment to long term relationships and having children. When Latinos interact with members of the larger gay and lesbian community some of the traditional values may be perceived as sexually, socially and politically conservative. However, the integration of an individual's cultural and sexual identity is often a difficult and lengthy process. In cases when this integration is not taking place, individuals may divorce their sexual identities (public) from their sexual behaviors (private).

HOMOSEXUALITY, SEXUAL IDENTITY, AND SEXUAL BEHAVIOR

In pre-Columbian times, homosexuality was common in the Americas and was a source of scandal to the Spanish conquerors, who could not understand its institutional nature. Lucena-Salmoval (1990, p. 76) describes how Cortes branded all the Mexicans along the Atlantic coast as sodomites: "We have seen and been informed that they are all sodomites and practice that abominable rite." The European Inquisition stopped homosexuality as it was known and practiced by different native cultures of the Americas before the Conquest. Catholic traditions and beliefs emerged as the strongest influence in the development of new sexual mores.

Catholic teachings, however, generated and reinforced contradictions and duality. The Marianista role, while emphasizing the sexual separation between the sexes, indirectly encourages closeness between individuals of the same gender. The double sex standard also encourages undisclosed bisexualism among some men and women. It is not infrequent for young Latinos/as to engage in same-gender behavior, beginning with adolescence (Caraballo-Dieguez, 1989; Espin, 1984). These types of contacts may continue as teenagers become adults.

Because of the already described sharply defined gender roles in Latino communities, the general belief is that feminine males are passive and penetrable, like females. Masculine males are active and impenetrable and the anus provides sexual pleasure like the vagina (Carrier, 1989). Thus, in the Latino communities it is important to make a clear distinction between sexual identity and sexual behavior. Sexual behavior among Latino men is defined by the "masculinity" of the act: Men who insert their penises are regarded as masculine; those who receive them are viewed as feminine and degraded (Paz, 1961). Same gender sexual contact is tolerated for men if it is seen as masculine.

After they marry, males may keep a "male mistress" as an alternative to the traditionally sanctioned female mistress. Married men usually do not feel that they are being unfaithful to their wives since they are involved with another male. Anonymous sex with men also may be an alternative for Latino men to channel their sexual impulses and desires to be sexually close to other men. These types of sexual contacts among males are impersonal, genital-centered, and deprived of any social or emotional involvement or support. Due to the undisclosed and unplanned nature of these practices, safer sex tends not to be a high priority. Separating sexual identity from sexual behavior allows men to maintain their socially prescribed Macho roles.

The limited development of a Latino lesbian and gay community may influence Latinas and Latinos to be more variable in their sexual orientation identity than White gay men and lesbians (Peterson & Marin, 1988). Research conducted in Mexico in the 1980s estimated that the percentage of males with mixed sexual histories may be as high as 30% or more for the 15-25 age group (Carrier, 1985). However, the number of Latino males exhibiting homosexual behavior and self-identifying as gay tends to be lower. "Macho" or "active" men do not see their "passive" or effeminate male partners necessarily as male. Thus, they do not perceive themselves as engaging in homosexual behavior. Passive males are often perceived as a third sex. The often used phrase with minority men: "Men who have sex with men" may not provide the right identifier for undisclosed bisexual Latino men.

Latino homosexuals or bisexuals, living within communities that are still heterosexually conservative, are culturally forced to opt for one of the two polarized heterosexual gender roles and adopt public heterosexual behavior. For them, unlike many White middle class men and women, there is no middle-of-the-road option (De La Vega, 1990). A homosexual Latino male may be *closeted* because he cannot adopt the transvestite or the publicly effeminate roles Latino communities accept and know. As with gender roles, males tend to adopt the male or macho role or the effeminate or female like role. Undisclosed bisexual behavior is thus culturally engendered and reinforced. Argueles and Rich (1984) synthesize these behaviors by using a popular Latin American saying: *se dice nada, se hace todo* (say nothing, do everything). For many Latino families discussing sexuality in general is taboo, let alone alternative expressions of sexuality (Rose, 1994). Although sexual diversity is part of all communities, there is a tendency towards not verbalizing or making it real. The unspoken does not exist. These practices present challenges to liberating strategies such as coming-out.

The described dichotomy experienced by males takes its own unique dimension with women. Latinos are less aware of the existence of lesbians than of gay men in their communities. Generally only the openly *butch* types (i.e., those violating gender roles) are recognized as lesbians (Espin, 1984; Tremble et al., 1989). Many Latina lesbians hide their sexual orientation to avoid stigmatization within their own ethnic communities (Amaro, 1978). Coming out for a Latina has been described as the ultimate rebellion against her culture through her sexual behavior. The Latino lesbian goes against two moral prohibitions: sexuality and homosexuality (Anzaldua, 1987). On the other hand, Latino cultures encourage closeness among women. Manifestations of affection between women are expected and accepted. It is not uncommon for heterosexual women to walk arm in arm or to hold hands in public. Kissing is the most common greeting between women in many Latino cultures. These cultural based practices often provide a space for hiding same gender attraction and for expressing intimacy and affection in public.

This described "Latino model" has shaped gay and lesbian couples to the image of heterosexual couples (Munoz, 1996). In the case of gay men, there is a tendency to assign roles between partners mirroring the very polarized Latino heterosexual gender roles. The more Latinos and Latinas have a chance to explore alternative models grounded in their own unique needs and strengths, the more alternative models will emerge. Latinas and

Latinos living in large urban centers are coming out of the closet in increasing numbers. When a family member's homosexuality is known, acceptance or accommodation is common among most Latino families. Concerned individuals and their family members may cope by resorting to a conspiracy of silence about homosexuality. In social functions with relatives and neighbors, families will treat homosexual household members as though they were heterosexual. Socioeconomic factors reinforce these cultural practices. Lacking the means to move out on their own or the need to stay and help support the family are also factors. Latina lesbians and Latino gay men that remain at home engage in a kind of culturally prescribed role playing. A social worker (an outsider) may not see beyond the role playing and believe that what she or he sees is the truth.

CHALLENGES AND STRATEGIES

The *machismo* and *marianismo* codes are not reinforced by the American culture, which has been more influenced by the women's movement. The feminist movement changed women's ideas about sexuality, raised questions about traditional gender roles, and reduced stigma surrounding lesbianism (Faderman, 1984; Krieger, 1982; Lockard, 1985). Traditional Latino conceptions of manhood and womanhood are changing toward a more egalitarian model due to increased access to formal education and exposure to American society (Torres-Martullo, 1980). However, factors such as national origin, socioeconomic status, educational level, rural versus urban, and acculturation status have to be considered when interpreting variance in levels of awareness and acceptance of lesbian and gay lifestyles among different Latino communities.

As gender roles are redefined in the Latino community lesbian and gay male identities are becoming a choice for increasing numbers of young people. They are breaking new ground in their communities. These young Latinas and Latinos are true pioneers in the process of integrating their ethnic and sexual identities. They need support from both the gay and the Latino communities. It is important to support young Latinos and Latinas in developing gay and lesbian identities that are culturally grounded. The lesbian and gay community will be doing a disservice to Latinos and the community by ignoring the central role ethnicity and culture play in the formation of sexual identities. When assessing the sexuality of a client, staying at the identity level will only provide part of the client's history. Her or his sexual behavior may not match her or his sexual identity. This issue becomes even more salient when the language and terminology used are not culturally specific.

From a developmental approach, Latinas and Latinos have to be respected for whom they are, sexually and ethnically. Interventions are needed to support the creation of new narratives honoring individual and collective stories of liberation from being oppressor or oppressed (Freire, 1995). To learn how to dream about a better future where a "familia" can be made up by two men or two women is an essential step in the process of integrating identities. Latino and Latina clients have to be able to integrate their unique cultural values and cosmologies into their lesbian and gay experience. For this integration to materialize, both communities need to be more generous with each other. When lesbian and gay communities and Latino communities unite around issues that oppress both communities, such as the HIV/AIDS pandemic, they will get to know each other better. It is through working in the political and social arenas that needed coalitions will be created. It is imperative that members of both communities are nurtured and cherished as whole people. It is time to reassess the world view guiding existing models and test them for cultural relevance. A cultural deficit approach can no longer be used to explain the lack of effectiveness in reaching Latino gays and Latina lesbians. It is time to accept different world views, listen to other voices and integrate culturally grounded practices. Social workers can play a vital role as "cultural mediators." The family and the community are the targets of social work interventions. Social workers can support indigenous leaders, promote democratic participation and representation in agencies, and support coalition building. The community of origin aspect of this journey needs to be rescued and dealt with and social workers need to avoid presenting individualism as the only viable avenue to becoming whole sexually.

REFERENCES

Amaro, H. (1978). "Coming out" conflicts for Hispanic lesbians. Paper presented at the National Coalition of Hispanic Mental Health and Human Service Organizations (COSMHO), Austin, TX (October 2, 1978).

Anzaldua, G. (1987). *Borderlands/La Frontera: The new mestiza.* San Francisco: Aunt Lute.

Arguelles, L., & Rich, R. (1984). Homosexuality, homophobia, and revolution: Notes towards an understanding of the Cuban lesbian and gay male experience, part I. *Signs, 9,* 686-702.

Blauner, R. (1976). *Racial oppression in America.* New York: Harper & Row.

Caraballo-Dieguez, A. (1989). Hispanic culture, gay male culture and AIDS: Counseling implications. *Journal of Counseling and Development, 68,* 26-30.

Carrier, J.M. (1985). Mexican male bisexuality. In F. Klein, & T. Wolf (Eds.), *Bisexualities theory and research.* New York: The Haworth Press, Inc.

Carrier, J.M. (1989). Sexual behavior and spread of AIDS in Mexico. *Medical Anthropology, 10,* 129-142.

Chan, C.S. (1989). Issues of identity development among Asian-American lesbians and gay men. *Journal of Counseling and Development, 68,* 16-18.

Comas-Díaz, L. (1987). Feminist therapy with mainland Puerto Rican women. *Psychology of Women Quarterly 11,* 461-474.

Davis, S., & Chavez, V. (1995). Hispanic househusbands. In A. Padilla (Ed.), *Hispanic psychology.* (pp. 257-270). Thousand Oaks, CA: Sage.

De la Cancela, V. (1981). Towards a critical psychological analysis of machismo: Puerto Ricans and mental health. *Dissertation Abstracts International* 42:368-B.

De la Vega, E. (1990). Considerations for reaching the Latino population. *SIECUS Report, 18,* 3-15. Sex Information and Education Council of the U.S.

Espin, O.M. (1984). Cultural and historical influences on sexuality in Hispanic/Latin women: Implications for psychotherapy. In C. Vance (Ed.), *Pleasure and danger: Exploring female sexuality* (pp. 149-163). London: Routledge & Kegan Paul.

Espiritu, Y. (1992). *Asian American panethnicity: Bridging institutions and identities.* Philadelphia: Temple University Press.

Faderman, L. (1981). The "new gay" lesbian. *Journal of Homosexuality, 10,* 85-95.

Foucault, M. (1990). *The history of sexuality.* New York: Vintage.

Freire, P. (1995). *Pedagogy of the oppressed.* New York: Continuum.

Freire, P. (1984). *Pedagogy of hope.* New York: Continuum.

Garnets, L., & Kimmel, D. (1991). Lesbian and gay male dimensions in the psychological study of human diversity. In Goodchilds, J.D. (Ed.), *Psychological Perspectives on Human Diversity in America* (pp. 143-190). Washington, DC: American Psychological Association.

Geschwender, J. (1992). Ethgender, women's waged labor, and economic mobility. *Social Problems, 39,* 1-6.

Gutman, M. C. (1996). *The meanings of macho: Being a man in Mexico City.* Berkeley, CA: University of California Press.

Icard, L. (1985/1986). Black gay men and conflicting social identities: Sexual orientation versus racial identity. *Journal of Social Work and Human Sexuality, 4,* 83-92.

Kanuha, V. (1990). Compounding the triple jeopardy: Battering in lesbian of color relationships. *Women & Therapy, 9,* 169-184.

Krieger, S. (1982). Lesbian identity and community: Recent social science literature. *Signs, 8,* 91-108.

Lockard, D. (1985). The lesbian community: An anthropological approach. *Journal of Homosexuality, 11,* 83-95.

Lucena-Salmoval, M. (1990). *America 1492: Portrait of a continent 500 years ago.* Milan-Italy: Anaya Editoriale.

Marin, G. (1989). AIDS prevention among Hispanics: Needs, risk behaviors, and cultural values. *Public Health Reports, 104,* 411-415.

Marsiglia, F. F., & Zorita, P. (1996). Narratives as a means to support Latino/a students in higher education. *Reflections, 2,* 54-62.

Morales, E. S. (1990). HIV infection and Hispanic gay and bisexual men. *Hispanic Journal of Behavioral Sciences, 12,* 212-222.

Munoz, C. B. (1996). *Uruguay homosexual: Culturas, minorias y discriminacion desde una sociologia de la homosexualidad.* Montevideo-Uruguay: Ediciones Trilce.

Oboler, S. (1995). *Ethnic labels, Latino lives, identity and the politics of (re)presentation in the United States.* Minneapolis: University of Minnesota Press.

Organista, K., Organista, P., Garcia de Alba, J., & Castillo Moran, M. (1996). AIDS and condom-related knowledge, beliefs, and behaviors in Mexican migrant laborers. *Hispanic Journal of Behavioral Science, 18,* 392-406.

Padilla, F. (1985). *Latino ethnic consciousness.* Notre Dame, IN: University of Notre Dame.

Paz, O. (1961). *The labyrinth of solitude: Life and thought in Mexico.* New York: Grove Press.

Peterson, J. L., & Marín, G. (1988). Issues in the prevention of AIDS among Black and Hispanic men. *American Psychologist, 88,* 871-957.

Rose, D. J. (1994, June 1). Coming out, standing out. *Hispanic, 21,* 44-48.

Rueschenberg, E., & Buriel, R. (1995). Mexican American family functioning and acculturation. In A. Padilla (Ed.), *Hispanic psychology* (pp. 15-25). Thousand Oaks, CA: Sage.

Stevens, E. (1973). Machismo and marianismo. *Transition-Society, 10,* 57-63.

Torres-Martullo. C. M. (1980). Acculturation, sex role values and mental health among Puerto Ricans in mainland United States. In M. Padilla (Ed.), *Acculturation: Theory, models and some new findings* (pp. 120-132). Boulder, CO: Westview Press.

Tremble, B., Schneider, M., & Appathurai, C. (1989). Growing up gay or lesbian in a multicultural context. *Journal of Homosexuality, 17,* 253-267.

Vygotsky, L. (1979). *Mind in society: The development of higher psychological processes.* Cambridge, Mass: Harvard University Press.

Wagenheim, K. (1970). *Puerto Rico: A profile.* New York: Praeger.

Woodman, W.S., Kawasaki, H., & Mayeda, R. (1983). Lifestyles and identity maintenance among gay Japanese-American males. *Alternative Lifestyles, 5,* 236-243.

Yep, G. (1995). Communicating the HIV/AIDS risk. In A. Padilla (Ed.), *Hispanic psychology* (pp. 196-227). Thousand Oaks, CA: Sage.

Zarestsky, E. (1976). *Capitalism: The family and personal life.* New York: Harper-Colophon.

Index

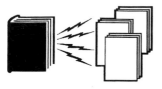

Haworth
DOCUMENT DELIVERY
SERVICE

This valuable service provides a single-article order form for any article from a Haworth journal.

- *Time Saving:* No running around from library to library to find a specific article.
- *Cost Effective:* All costs are kept down to a minimum.
- *Fast Delivery:* Choose from several options, including same-day FAX.
- *No Copyright Hassles:* You will be supplied by the original publisher.
- *Easy Payment:* Choose from several easy payment methods.

Open Accounts Welcome for ...
- Library Interlibrary Loan Departments
- Library Network/Consortia Wishing to Provide Single-Article Services
- Indexing/Abstracting Services with Single Article Provision Services
- Document Provision Brokers and Freelance Information Service Providers

---

MAIL or *FAX* THIS ENTIRE ORDER FORM TO:

Haworth Document Delivery Service
The Haworth Press, Inc.
10 Alice Street
Binghamton, NY 13904-1580

or FAX: 1-800-895-0582
or CALL: 1-800-429-6784
9am-5pm EST

PLEASE SEND ME PHOTOCOPIES OF THE FOLLOWING SINGLE ARTICLES:
1) Journal Title: _____
 Vol/Issue/Year: _____ Starting & Ending Pages: _____
Article Title: _____
_____

2) Journal Title: _____
 Vol/Issue/Year: _____ Starting & Ending Pages: _____
Article Title: _____
_____

3) Journal Title: _____
 Vol/Issue/Year: _____ Starting & Ending Pages: _____
Article Title: _____
_____

4) Journal Title: _____
 Vol/Issue/Year: _____ Starting & Ending Pages: _____
Article Title: _____
_____

(See other side for Costs and Payment Information)

COSTS: Please figure your cost to order quality copies of an article.

1. Set-up charge per article: $8.00
   ($8.00 × number of separate articles) _____

2. Photocopying charge for each article:

   1-10 pages: $1.00 _____

   11-19 pages: $3.00 _____

   20-29 pages: $5.00 _____

   30+ pages: $2.00/10 pages _____

3. Flexicover (optional): $2.00/article _____

4. Postage & Handling: US: $1.00 for the first article/
   $.50 each additional article _____

   Federal Express: $25.00 _____

   Outside US: $2.00 for first article/
   $.50 each additional article _____

5. Same-day FAX service: $.50 per page _____

GRAND TOTAL: _____

METHOD OF PAYMENT: (please check one)

❏ Check enclosed   ❏ Please ship and bill. PO # _____
   (sorry we can ship and bill to bookstores only! All others must pre-pay)

❏ Charge to my credit card: ❏ Visa; ❏ MasterCard; ❏ Discover;
   ❏ American Express;

Account Number: _____ Expiration date: _____

Signature: *X* _____

Name: _____ Institution: _____

Address: _____

_____

City: _____ State: _____ Zip: _____

Phone Number: _____ FAX Number: _____

MAIL or *FAX* THIS ENTIRE ORDER FORM TO:

Haworth Document Delivery Service | **or FAX:** 1-800-895-0582
The Haworth Press, Inc. | **or CALL:** 1-800-429-6784
10 Alice Street | (9am-5pm EST)
Binghamton, NY 13904-1580